# CREDO PERSPECTIVES

VOLUMES ALREADY PUBLISHED

RENÉ DUBOS: THE TORCH OF LIFE

R. M. MAC IVER: THE CHALLENGE OF THE
    PASSING YEARS

F. S. C. NORTHROP: MAN, NATURE AND GOD

MOSES HADAS: OLD WINE, NEW BOTTLES

ERICH FROMM: BEYOND THE CHAINS OF ILLUSION

WILLIAM O. DOUGLAS: THE ANATOMY OF LIBERTY

HANS KOHN: LIVING IN A WORLD REVOLUTION

JAMES BRYANT CONANT: TWO MODES OF THOUGHT

POPE PAUL VI: DIALOGUES

FRED HOYLE: ENCOUNTER WITH THE FUTURE

MARTIN C. D'ARCY, S.J.: DIALOGUE WITH MYSELF

HERBERT READ: THE REDEMPTION OF THE ROBOT

EDMUND W. SINNOTT: THE BRIDGE OF LIFE

POPE JOHN XXIII: AN INVITATION TO HOPE

PAUL TILLICH: MY SEARCH FOR ABSOLUTES

MARTIN BUBER: A BELIEVING HUMANISM

JAMES JOHNSON SWEENEY: VISION AND IMAGE

CREDO PERSPECTIVES

FOUNDED AND PLANNED BY
RUTH NANDA ANSHEN

BEYOND THE CHAINS OF ILLUSION

*My Encounter
with Marx and Freud*

by ERICH FROMM

A TOUCHSTONE BOOK
Published by Simon & Schuster, Inc.
NEW YORK

Copyright © 1962 by Simon & Schuster, Inc.
Introduction to the Credo Perspectives series © 1962 by Ruth Nanda Anshen

This Touchstone Edition, 1985
Published by Simon & Schuster, Inc.
Simon & Schuster Building
Rockefeller Center
1230 Avenue of the Americas
New York, New York 10020
TOUCHSTONE and colophon are registered trademarks of
Simon & Schuster, Inc.
Manufactured in the United States of America
10 9 8 7 6 5 4 3 2 1
10 9 8 7 6 5 4 3 2 1 Pbk.
Library of Congress Cataloging in Publication Data
Fromm, Erich, 1900–
   Beyond the chains of illusion.
   (A Touchstone book)
   Reprint. Originally published: New York: Simon & Schuster, 1962.
   1. Marx, Karl, 1818-1883. 2. Freud, Sigmund, 1856-
1939. I. Title.
B3305.M74F72   1985   150.19'5   84-27730
ISBN 0-671-08535-2
ISBN 0-671-20862-4 Pbk.

Contents

CREDO PERSPECTIVES
Their Meaning and Function
RUTH NANDA ANSHEN   vii

I	Some Personal Antecedents	3
II	The Common Ground	13
III	The Concept of Man and His Nature	27
IV	Human Evolution	33
V	Human Motivation	38
VI	The Sick Individual and the Sick Society	43
VII	The Concept of Mental Health	63
VIII	Individual and Social Character	71
IX	The Social Unconscious	88
X	The Fate of Both Theories	133
XI	Some Related Ideas	149
XII	Credo	174

CREDO PERSPECTIVES

Their Meaning and Function

Credo Perspectives suggest that twentieth-century man is living in one of the world's most challenging periods, unprecedented in history, a dynamic period when he has almost unlimited choices for good and evil. In all civilizations of the world of our modern epoch, in both socialistic and capitalistic societies, we are faced with the compelling need to understand more clearly the forces that dominate our world and to modify our attitudes and behavior accordingly. And this will only happen if our best minds are persuaded and assembled to concentrate on the nature of this new epoch in evolutionary and moral history. For we are confronted with a very basic change. Man has intervened in the evolutionary process and he must better appreciate this fact with its influence on his life and work, and then try to develop the wisdom to direct the process, to recognize the mutable and the immutable elements in his moral nature and the relationship between freedom and order.

The authors in this series declare that science now permits us to say that "objective" nature, the world which alone is "real" to us as the one in which we all, scientists

included, are born, love, hate, work, reproduce and die,
is the world given us by our senses and our minds—a
world in which the sun crosses the sky from east to west,
a world of three-dimensional space, a world of values which
we, and we alone, must make. It is true that scientific
knowledge about macroscopic or subatomic events may
enable us to perform many acts we were unable to perform before. But it is as inhabitants of this human world
that we perform them and must finally recognize that there
is a certain kind of scientific "objectivity" that can lead us
to know everything but to understand nothing.

The symbol of *Credo Perspectives* is the Eye of Osiris.
It is the inner eye. Man sees in two ways: with his physical
eyes, in an empirical sensing or *seeing* by direct observation, and also by an indirect envisaging. He possesses in
addition to his two sensing eyes a single, image-making,
spiritual and intellectual Eye. And it is the *in-sight* of this
inner Eye that purifies and makes sacred our understanding
of the nature of things; for that which was shut fast has
been opened by the command of the inner Eye. And we
become aware that to believe is to see.

This series is designed to present a kind of intellectual
autobiography of each author, to portray the nature and
meaning of his creative process and to show the relevance
of his work to his feelings and aspirations. In it we hope
also to reflect the influence of the work on the man and
on society, and to point to the freedom, or lack of freedom,
to choose and pursue one profession rather than another.
For the creator in any realm must surrender himself to a
passionate pursuit of his labors, guided by deep personal
intimations of an as yet undiscovered reality.

Credo Perspectives hope to unlock a consciousness that at first sight may seem to be remote but is proved on acquaintance to be surprisingly immediate, since it stems from the need to reconcile the life of action with the life of contemplation, of practice with principle, of thought with feeling, of knowing with being. For the whole meaning of *self* lies within the observer, and its shadow is cast naturally on the object observed. The divorce of man from his work, the division of man into an eternal and temporal half, results in an estrangement of man from his creative source, and ultimately from his fellows and from himself.

The hope of this series is to suggest that the universe itself is a vast entity where man will be lost if it does not converge in the person; for material forces or energies, or impersonal ideals, or scientifically objectified learning are meaningless without their relevance for human life and their power to disclose, even in the dark tendencies of man's nature, a law transcending man's arbitrariness.

For the personal is a far higher category than the abstract universal. Personality itself is an emotional, not an intellectual, experience; and the greatest achievement of knowledge is to combine the personal within a larger unity, just as in the higher stages of development the parts that make up the whole acquire greater and greater independence and individuality within the context of the whole. Reality itself is the harmony which gives to the component particulars of a thing the equilibrium of the whole. And while physical observations are ordered with direct reference to the experimental conditions, we have in sensate experience to do with separate observations whose correla-

tion can only be indicated by their belonging to the wholeness of mind.

It is the endeavor of the authors to show that man has
reached a turning point in consciousness, that his relationship with his creativity demands a clarification that can
widen and deepen his understanding of the nature of reality. Work is made for man, not man for work. This series
hopes to demonstrate the sacramental character of work,
which is more easily achieved when the principal objects
of our attention have taken on a symbolic form that is
generally recognized and accepted; and this suggests a *law*
in the relationship of a person and his chosen discipline:
that it is valuable only when the spiritual, the creative, life
is strong enough to insist on some expression through
symbols. For no work can be based on material, techno-
logical, historical, or physical aspirations alone.

The human race is now entering upon a new phase of
evolutionary consciousness and progress, a phase in which,
impelled by the forces of evolution itself, it must converge
upon itself and convert itself into one single human organ-
ism infused by a reconciliation of knowing and being in
their inner unity and destined to make a qualitative leap
into a higher form of consciousness that would transcend
and complement individual consciousness as we know it,
or otherwise destroy itself. For the entire universe is one
vast field, potential for incarnation and achieving incan-
descence here and there of reason and spirit. And in the
whole world of *quality* with which by the nature of our
minds we necessarily make contact, we here and there
apprehend pre-eminent value. This can be achieved only
if we recognize that we are unable to focus our attention

on the particulars of a whole without diminishing our comprehension of the whole, and of course, conversely, we can focus on the whole only by diminishing our comprehension of the particulars which constitute the whole.

The kind of knowledge afforded by mathematical physics ever since the seventeenth century has come more and more to furnish mankind with an ideal for all knowledge. This error about the nature of knowledge it is the hope of this series to expose. For knowledge is a process, not a product and the results of scientific investigation do not carry with them self-evident implications. There are now, however, signs of new centers of resistance among men everywhere in almost all realms of knowledge. Many share the conviction that a deep-seated moral and philosophical reform is needed concerning our understanding of the nature of man and the nature of knowledge in relation to the work man is performing, in relation to his *credo* and his life.

Credo Perspectives constitute an endeavor to alter the prevailing conceptions, not only of the nature of knowledge and work, but also of creative achievements in general, as well as of the human agent who inquires and creates, and of the entire fabric of the culture formed by such activities. In other words, this is an endeavor to show that what we see and what we do are no more and no less than what we are.

It is the endeavor of *Credo Perspectives* to define the new reality in which the estrangement of man from his work, resulting in the self-estrangement in man's existence, is overcome. This new reality is born through the reconciliation of what a man *knows* with what a man *is*. Being itself in all its presuppositions and implications can only be understood through the totality, through wholeness. St. Paul, who, like Isaiah before him, went into the marketplace not to secularize truth but to proclaim it, taught man that the "new creation" could be explained only by conquering the daemonic cleavages, the destructive split, in soul and cosmos. And that fragmentation always destroys a unity, produces a tearing away from the source and thereby creates disunity and isolation. The fruit can never be separated from the tree. The Tree of Life can never be disjoined from the Tree of Knowledge for both have *one and the same* root. And if man allows himself to fall into isolation, if he seeks to maintain a self segregated from the totality of which he is a necessary part, if he chooses to be unrelated to the original context of all created things in which he too has his place—including his own labors— then this act of apostasy bears fruit in the demiurgical presumption of *magic,* a form of animism in which man seeks an authority of the self, placing himself above the law of the universe by attempting to separate the inseparable. He thus creates an unreal world after having destroyed or deserted the real. And in this way the method of analysis, of scientific objectivity, which is good and necessary in its right place, is endowed with a destructive power when it is allowed to usurp a place for which it is not fitted.

The naturalist principle that man is the measure of all things has been shattered more than ever in our own age by the question, "What is the measure of man?" Postmodern man is more profoundly perplexed about the nature of man than his ancestors were. He is on the verge of spiritual and moral insanity. He does not know who he is.

And having lost the sense of who and what he is, he fails to grasp the meaning of his fellow man, of his vocation and of the nature and purpose of knowledge itself. For what is not understood cannot be known. And it is this cognitive faculty which is frequently abrogated by the "scientific" theory of knowledge, a theory that refuses to recognize the existence of comprehensive entities as distinct from their particulars. The central act of knowing is indeed that form of comprehension which is never absent from any process of knowing and is finally its ultimate sanction.

Science itself acknowledges as real a host of entities that cannot be described completely in materialistic or mechanistic terms, and it is this transcendence out of the domain of science into a region from which science itself can be appraised that *Credo Perspectives* hope to define. For the essence of the ebb and flow of experience, of sensations, the richness of the immediacy of directly apprehended knowledge, the metaphysical substance of what assails our being, is the very act itself of sensation and affection and therefore must escape the net of rational analysis, yet is intimately related to every cognitive act. It is this increasing intellectual climate that is calling into birth once more the compelling Socratic questions, "What is the purpose of life, the meaning of work?" "What is man?" Plato himself could give us only an indirect answer: "Man is declared to be that creature who is constantly in search of himself, a creature who at every moment of his existence must examine and scrutinize the conditions of his existence. He is a being in search of meaning."

From this it is evident that there is present in the universe a *law* applicable to all nature including man and his work. Life itself then is seen to be a creative process elaborating and maintaining *order* out of the randomness of matter, endlessly generating new and unexpected structures and properties by building up associations that qualitatively transcend their constituent parts. This is not to diminish the importance of "scientific objectivity." It is, however, to say that the mind possesses a quality that cannot be isolated or known exclusively in the sense of objective knowledge. For it consists in that elusive humanity in us, our self, that knows. It is that inarticulate awareness that includes and *comprehends* all we know. It consists in the irreducible active voice of man and is recognized only in other things, only when the circle of consciousness closes around its universe of events.

Our hope is to point to a new dimension of morality— not that of constraint and prohibition but a morality that lies as a fountainhead within the human soul, a morality of aspiration to spiritual experience. It suggests that necessity is laid upon us to infer entities that are not observed and are not observable. For an unseen universe is necessary to explain the seen. The flux is seen, but to account for its structure and its nature we infer particles of various kinds to serve as the vertices of the changing patterns, placing less emphasis on the isolated units and more on the structure and nature of relations. The process of knowing involves an immaterial becoming, an immaterial identification, and finally, knowledge itself is seen to be a dependent variable of immateriality. And somewhere along this spiritual pilgrimage man's pure observation is relinquished and gives way to the deeper experience of awe, for there can be no explanation of a phenomenon by searching for its origin but only by discerning its immanent law—this quality of transcendence that abides even in matter itself. The present situation in the world and the vast accretion of knowledge have produced a serious anxiety which may be overcome by re-evaluating the character, kinship, logic and operation of man in relation to his work. For work implies goals and intimately affects the person performing the work. Therefore the correlation and relatedness of ideas, facts and values that are in perpetual interplay could emerge from these volumes as they point to the inner synthesis and organic unity of man and his labors. For though no labor alone can enrich the person, no enrichment can be achieved without absorbing and intense labor. We then experience a unity of faith, labor and grace which prepares the mind for receiving a truth from sources over which it has no control. This is especially true since the great challenge of our age arises out of man's inventions in relation to his life.

Thus *Credo Perspectives* seek to encourage the perfection not only of man's works but also and above all the fulfillment of himself as a person. And so we now are summoned to consider not only man in the process of development as a human subject but also his influence on the object of his investigation and creation. Observation alone is interference. The naïve view that we can observe any system and predict its behavior without altering it by the very act of observation was an unjustified extrapolation from Newton's *Celestial Mechanics*. We can observe the moon or even a satellite and predict its behavior without perhaps appreciably interfering with it, but we cannot do this with an amoeba, far less with a man and still less with a society of men. It is the heart of the question of the nature of work itself. If we regard our labors as a process of shaping or forming, then the fruits of our labors play the part of a mold by which we ourselves are shaped. And this means, in the preservation of the identity of the knower and the known, that cognition and generation, that is, creation, though in different spheres, are nevertheless alike.

It is hoped that the influence of such a series may help to overcome the serious separations between function and meaning and may show that the extraordinary crisis through which the world is passing can be fruitfully met by recognizing that knowledge has not been completely dehumanized and has not totally degenerated into a mere notebook overcrowded with formulas that few are able to understand or apply.

For mankind is now engaged in composing a new theme. Life never manifests itself in negative terms. And our hope lies in drawing from every category of work a conviction that nonmaterial values can be discovered in positive, affirmative, visible things. The estrangement between the temporal and nontemporal man is coming to an end, community is inviting communion, and a vision of the human condition more worthy of man is engendered, connecting ever more closely the creative mind with the currents of spiritual energy which breaks for us the bonds of habit and keeps us in touch with the permanence of being through our work.

And as, long ago, the Bearers of Bread were succeeded by the Bearers of Torches, so now, in the immediacies of life, it is the image of man and his vocation that can rekindle the high passion of humanity in its quest for light.

Refusing to divorce work from life or love from knowledge, it is action, it is passion that enhances our being.

We live in an expanding universe and also in the moral infinite of that other universe, the universe of man. And along the whole stretched arc of this universe we may see that extreme limit of complicity where reality seems to shape itself within the work man has chosen for his realization. Work then becomes not only a way of knowledge, it becomes even more a way of life—of life in its totality. For the last end of every maker is himself.

"And the places that have been desolate for ages shall be built in thee: thou shalt raise up the foundations of generation and generation; and thou shalt be called the repairer of the fences, turning the paths into rest."*

RUTH NANDA ANSHEN

Kind of
pathetic

girl...
isn't she?

---

* Isaiah, 58:12.

"The demand to give up the illusions about its condition is the demand to give up a condition which needs illusions."

"Criticism has plucked the imaginary flowers from the chain not so that man will wear the chain without any fantasy or consolation but so that he will shake off the chain and cull the living flower."

KARL MARX.

"Men can not remain children forever; they must in the end go out into 'hostile life.' We may call this 'education to reality.'"

"No, our science is no illusion. But an illusion it would be to suppose that what science can not give us we can get elsewhere."

"Where there is Id, there shall be Ego."

SIGMUND FREUD.

BEYOND THE CHAINS OF ILLUSION
My Encounter with Marx and Freud

I

SOME PERSONAL ANTECEDENTS

IF A MAN asks himself how he ever became interested in those fields of thought which were destined to occupy the most important place throughout his life, he will not find it easy to give a simple answer. Perhaps he was born with an inclination for certain questions, or perhaps it was the influence of certain teachers, or of current ideas, or of personal experiences which led him along the path of his later interests—who knows which of these factors have determined the course of his life? Indeed, if one wanted to know precisely the relative weight of all these factors, nothing short of a detailed historical autobiography could even attempt to give the answers.

Since the purpose of this book is by no means that of a historical, but rather that of an intellectual autobiography, I shall try to pick out a few experiences during my adolescence which led to my later interest in the theories of Freud and of Marx, and the relation between the two.

If I want to understand how the problem of why people act the way they do became of such paramount interest to me, it might be sufficient to assume that having been an only child, with an anxious and moody father and a depression-prone mother was enough to arouse my in-

3

terest in the strange and mysterious reasons for human reactions. Yet, I vividly remember one incident—I must have been around twelve years old—which stimulated my thoughts far beyond those I had had before and which prepared an interest in Freud which was to become manifest only ten years later.

This was the incident: I had known a young woman, a friend of the family. Maybe she was twenty-five years of age; she was beautiful, attractive and in addition a painter, the first painter I ever knew. I remember having heard that she had been engaged but after some time had broken the engagement; I remember that she was almost invariably in the company of her widowed father. As I remember him, he was an old, uninteresting, and rather unattractive-looking man, or so I thought (maybe my judgment was somewhat biased by jealousy). Then one day I heard the shocking news: her father had died, and immediately afterwards she had killed herself and left a will which stipulated that she wanted to be buried together with her father.

I had never heard of an Oedipus complex or of incestuous fixations between daughter and father. But I was deeply touched. I had been quite attracted to the young woman; I had loathed the unattractive father; never before had I known anyone to commit suicide. I was hit by the thought "How is it possible?" How is it possible that a beautiful young woman should be so in love with her father, that she prefers to be buried with him to being alive to the pleasures of life and of painting?

Certainly I knew no answer, but the "how is it possible" stuck. And when I became acquainted with Freud's theories, they seemed to be the answer to a puzzling and frightening experience at a time when I was beginning to develop into an adolescent.

My interest in Marx's ideas has quite a different background. I was brought up in a religious Jewish family, and the writings of the Old Testament touched me and exhilarated me more than anything else I was exposed to. Not all of them to the same degree; I was bored by or even disliked the history of the conquest of Canaan by the Hebrews; I had no use for the stories of Mordecai or Esther; nor did I—at that time—appreciate the Song of Songs. But the story of Adam and Eve's disobedience, of Abraham's pleading with God for the salvation of the inhabitants of Sodom and Gomorrah, of Jonah's mission to Nineveh, and many other parts of the Bible impressed me deeply. But more than anything else, I was moved by the prophetic writings, by Isaiah, Amos, Hosea; not so much by their warnings and their announcement of disaster, but by their promise of the "end of days," when nations "shall beat their swords into plowshares and their spears into pruning hooks: nation shall not lift sword against nation, neither shall they learn war any more;" when all nations will be friends, and when "the earth shall be full of the knowledge of the Lord, as the waters cover the sea." The vision of universal peace and harmony between all nations touched me deeply when I was twelve and thirteen years old. Probably the immediate reason for this absorption by the idea of peace and internationalism is to be found in the situation in which I found myself: a Jewish boy in a Christian environment, experiencing small episodes of anti-Semitism but, more importantly, a feeling of strangeness and of clannishness on both sides. I disliked clannishness, maybe all the more so because I had an overwhelming wish to transcend the emotional isolation of a lonely, pampered boy; what could be more exciting and beautiful to me than the prophetic vision of universal brotherhood and peace?

Perhaps all these personal experiences would not have affected me so deeply and lastingly had it not been for the event that determined more than anything else my development: the First World War. When the war started during the summer of 1914, I was a fourteen-year-old boy for whom the excitement of war, the celebration of victories, the tragedy of the death of individual soldiers I knew, were uppermost in my experience. I was not concerned with the problem of war as such; I was not struck by its senseless inhumanity. But soon all this changed. Some experiences with my teachers helped. My Latin teacher, who in his lessons during the two years before the war had proclaimed as his favorite maxim the sentence, "Si vis pacem para bellum" (if you want peace prepare for war), showed his delight when the war broke out. I recognized that his alleged concern for peace could not have been true. How was it possible that a man who always seemed to have been so concerned with the preservation of peace should now be so jubilant about the war? From then on, I found it difficult to believe in the principle that armament preserves peace, even when advocated by people possessing more goodwill and honesty than my Latin teacher had.

I was equally struck by the hysteria of hate against the British which swept throughout Germany in those years. Suddenly they had become cheap mercenaries, evil and unscrupulous, trying to destroy our innocent and all-too-trusting German heroes. In the midst of this national hysteria, one decisive event stands out in my mind. In our English class we had been given the assignment of learning by heart the British national anthem. This assignment was given us before the summer vacation, while there was still peace. When classes were resumed we boys, partly out of mischief and partly because we were infected by the "hate England" mood, told the teacher that we refused to learn the national anthem of what was now our worst enemy. I still see him standing in front of the class, answering our protests with an ironical smile, and saying calmly: "Don't kid yourselves; so far England has never lost a war!" Here was the voice of sanity and realism in the midst of insane hatred—and it was the voice of a respected and admired teacher! This one sentence and the calm, rational way in which it was said, was an enlightenment. It broke through the crazy pattern of hate and national self-glorification and made me wonder and think, "How is it possible?"

I grew older and my doubts increased. A number of my uncles and cousins and older schoolmates were killed in the war; the victory forecasts of the generals proved to be wrong—and soon I learned to understand the double talk of "strategic retreats" and "victorious defense." And something else happened. The German press had from the very beginning described the war as one forced upon the German people by envious neighbors who wanted to strangle Germany in order to get rid of a successful rival. The war was described as a fight for freedom; was Germany not fighting against the very embodiment of slavery and oppression—the Russian Czar?

While all this sounded convincing for a while, especially since there was no voice of dissent to be heard, my belief in these assertions began to be assailed by doubts. First of all, there was the fact that an increasing number of socialist deputies voted against the war budget in the Reichstag and spoke critically against the German government's official position. A pamphlet was circulated privately entitled "J'accuse" (I accuse), which discussed the question of the war guilt essentially—as far as I remember—from the standpoint of the Western allies. It showed that the Imperial government was by no means the innocent victim of an attack but, together with the

Austian-Hungarian government, it was largely responsible for the war.

The war went on. The trenches extended from the
Swiss border north to the sea. One spoke with soldiers
and learned about the life they were leading boxed up in
the trenches and dugouts, exposed to concentrated artil-
lery fire which initiated an enemy attack, then trying again
and again to break through, and never succeeding. Year
after year the healthy men of each nation, living like animals in caves, killed each other with rifles, hand grenades,
machine guns, bayonets; the slaughter continued, accompanied by false promises of a speedy victory, false protestations of one's own innocence, false accusations against the
devilish enemy, false offers of peace, and insincere an-
nunciations of conditions for peace.

The longer this lasted, the more I changed from a
child to a man, the more urgent became the question
"How is it possible?" How is it possible that millions
of men continue to stay in the trenches, to kill innocent
men of other nations, and to be killed and thus to cause
the deepest pain to parents, wives, friends? What are they
fighting for? How is it possible that both sides believe
they are fighting for peace and freedom? How was it
possible for a war to break out when everybody claimed
that they did not want it? How is it possible that the war
continues when both sides claim they do not want any
conquests, but only the preservation of their respective
national possessions and integrity? If, as the following
events showed, both sides wanted conquests and fame for
their political and military leaders, how was it possible
that millions allowed themselves to be slaughtered on
both sides for the sake of some territory and the vanity of
some leaders? Is the war a result of a senseless accident,
or is it a result of certain social and political developments which follow their own laws and which can be

understood—or even predicted—provided one knows the nature of these laws?

When the war ended in 1918, I was a deeply troubled young man who was obsessed by the question of how war was possible, by the wish to understand the irrationality of human mass behavior, by a passionate desire for peace and international understanding. More, I had become deeply suspicious of all official ideologies and declarations, and filled with the conviction "of all one must doubt."

I have tried to show which experiences during my adolescence created the conditions for my passionate interest in the teachings of Freud and of Marx. I was deeply troubled by questions with regard to individual and social phenomena, and I was eager for an answer. I found answers both in Freud's and in Marx's systems. But I was also stimulated by the contrasts between the two systems and by the wish to solve these contradictions. Eventually, the older I grew and the more I studied, the more I doubted certain assumptions within the two systems. My main interest was clearly mapped out. I wanted to understand the laws that govern the life of the individual man, and the laws of society—that is, of men in their social existence. I tried to see the lasting truth in Freud's concepts as against those assumptions which were in need of revision. I tried to do the same with Marx's theory, and finally I tried to arrive at a synthesis which followed from the understanding and the criticism of both thinkers. This endeavor did not take place solely by means of theoretical speculation. Not that I think little of pure speculation (it all depends on who speculates); but believing in the superior value of blending empirical observation with speculation (much of the trouble with modern social science is that it often contains empirical observations without speculation), I have always tried to let my thinking be guided by the observation of facts and have striven to revise my theories when the observation seemed to warrant it.

As far as my psychological theories are concerned, I have had an excellent observation point. For over thirty-five years I have been a practicing psychoanalyst. I have examined minutely the behavior, the free associations, and the dreams of the people whom I have psychoanalyzed. There is not a single theoretical conclusion about man's psyche, either in this or in my other writings, which is not based on a critical observation of human behavior carried out in the course of this psychoanalytic work. As far as my study of social behavior is concerned, I have been less of an active participant than I was in my psychoanalytic practice. While I have been passionately interested in politics since the age of eleven or twelve (when I talked politics with a socialist who worked in my father's business) to this day, I have also known that I was temperamentally not suited for political activity. Thus I did not participate in any until recently, when I joined the American Socialist Party and became active in the peace movement. I did this not because I had changed my opinion with regard to my abilities, but because I felt it to be my duty not to remain passive in a world which seems to be moving toward a self-chosen catastrophe. I hasten to add that there was more to it than a sense of obligation. The more insane and dehumanized this world of ours seems to become, the more may an individual feel the need of being together and of working together with men and women who share one's human concerns. I certainly felt that need and have been grateful for the stimulating and encouraging companionship of those with whom I have had the good fortune of working. But even though I was not an active participant in politics, neither has my sociological thought been based entirely on books.

Indeed, without Marx and, to a lesser extent, other path-finders in sociology, my thinking would have been deprived of its most important stimuli. But the historical period through which I lived became a social laboratory which never failed. The First World War, the German and Russian revolutions, the victory of Fascism in Italy, and the slowly approaching victory of Nazism in Germany, the decay and perversion of the Russian revolution, the Spanish Civil War, the Second World War, and the armament race—all this offered a field of empirical observation which permitted the formation of hypotheses and their verification or rejection. Being passionately interested in the understanding of political events, and always realizing that by temperament I was not made to be active in them, I had a certain degree of objectivity even though never the dispassionateness which some political scientists believe to be a requisite of objectivity.

Thus far I have tried to enable the reader to share with me some of the experiences and thoughts which made me eagerly receptive when I came in touch with Freud's and Marx's ideas in my twenties. In the following pages I want to leave aside the reference to my personal development and speak about ideas and theoretical concepts: those of Freud and those of Marx, the contradictions between them, and my own ideas of a synthesis which springs from the attempt to understand and solve these contradictions.

There is, however, a need for one more remark before I start discussing the systems of Marx and Freud. Together with Einstein, Marx and Freud were the architects of the modern age. All three were imbued with the conviction of the fundamental orderliness of reality, the basic attitude which sees in the workings of nature—of which man is a part—not merely secrets to be discovered but pattern and design to be explored. Therefore their work, each in its own unique way, partakes of the elements of the highest art, as well as science, the highest expression of man's craving to understand, his need to know. My concern in this book, however, is only with Marx and Freud. By putting their names together the impression might easily arise that I consider them as two men of equal stature and equal historical significance. I want to make it clear at the outset that this is not so. That Marx is a figure of world historical significance with whom Freud cannot even be compared in this respect hardly needs to be said. Even if one, as I do, deeply regrets the fact that a distorted and degraded "Marxism" is preached in almost one-third of the world, this fact does not diminish the unique historical significance of Marx. But quite aside from this historical fact, I consider Marx, the thinker, as being of much greater depth and scope than Freud. Marx was capable of connecting a spiritual heritage of the enlightenment humanism and German idealism with the reality of economic and social facts, and thus to lay the foundations for a new science of man and society which is empirical and at the same time filled with the spirit of the Western humanist tradition. In spite of the fact that this spirit of humanism is negated and distorted by most of the systems which claim to speak in the name of Marx, I believe, as I shall try to show in this book, that a renaissance of Western humanism will restore to Marx his outstanding place in the history of human thought. But even when all this is said, it would be naive to ignore Freud's importance because he did not reach the heights of Marx. He is the founder of a truly scientific psychology, and his discovery of unconscious processes and of the dynamic nature of character traits is a unique contribution to the science of man which has altered the picture of man for all time to come.

II

THE COMMON GROUND

BEFORE ENTERING into the discussion of the details of Marx's and Freud's theories, I wish to describe in a brief sketch the fundamental premises common to both thinkers, the common soil, as it were, from which their thinking grows.

These fundamental ideas can best be expressed in three short statements, two of them Roman, one Christian. These statements are: 1) *De omnibus es dubitandum* (Of all one must doubt). 2) *Nihil humanum a mihi alienum puto* * (I believe nothing human to be alien to me).[1] 3) *The truth shall make you free.*

The first saying expresses what might be called "the critical mood." This mood is characteristic of modern science. But while in the natural sciences the doubt refers mainly to the evidence of the senses, hearsay, and traditional opinions, in Marx's and Freud's thinking the doubt refers particularly to man's thoughts about himself and about others. As I shall try to show in detail in the chapter on consciousness, Marx believed that most

---

* (Terentius)

[1] These two statements were mentioned by Marx as being his two favorite maxims. See in E. Fromm *Marx's Concept of Man* (New York: Frederick Ungar Publishing Co., Inc., 1961).

of what we think about ourselves and others is sheer illusion, is "ideology." He believed that our individual thoughts are patterned after the ideas any given society develops, and that these ideas are determined by the particular structure and mode of functioning of the society. A watchful, skeptical, doubting attitude toward all ideologies, ideas, and ideals, is characteristic for Marx. He always suspected them as veiling economic and social interests, and his skepticism was so strong that he could hardly ever use words like freedom, truth, justice—precisely because of the fact that they lend themselves to so much misuse, and not because freedom, justice, truth, were not the supreme values for him.

Freud thought in the same "critical mood." His whole psychoanalytic method could be described as "the art of doubting." Having been impressed by certain hypnotic experiments which demonstrated to what extent a person in a trance can believe in the reality of what is obviously not real, he discovered that most of the ideas of persons who are not in a trance also do not correspond to reality, and that on the other hand most of that which is real is not conscious. Marx thought the basic reality to be the socio-economic structure of society, while Freud believed it to be the libidinal organization of the individual. Yet they both had the same implacable distrust of the clichés, ideas, rationalizations, and ideologies which fill people's minds and which form the basis of what they mistake for reality.

This skepticism toward "common thought" is insolubly connected with a belief in the liberating force of truth. Marx wanted to liberate man from the chains of dependency, from alienation, from slavery to the economy. What was his method? Not, as is widely believed, force. He wanted to win the minds of the majority of the people.

While force, according to him, might be used if the
minority were to resist by force the will of the majority,
the main question for Marx was not the mechanism of
how to attain power in the state, but how to win the minds
of the people. In his "propaganda," Marx and his legitimate successors used the opposite method from the one
used by all other politicians, whether bourgeois, fascist,
or communist. He wanted to influence not by demagogic
persuasion, creating semi-hypnotic states supported by
fear of terror, but by an appeal to the sense of reality,
by truth. The assumption underlying Marx's "weapon of
truth" is the same as with Freud: that man lives with
illusions because these illusions make the misery of real
life bearable. If he can recognize the illusions for what
they are, that is to say, if he can wake up from the half-
dream state, then he can come to his senses, become aware
of his proper forces and powers, and change reality in such
a way that illusions are no longer necessary. "False consciousness," that is to say, the distorted picture of reality,
weakens man. Being in touch with reality, having an adequate picture of it, makes him stronger. Hence Marx believed that his most important weapon was truth, the
uncovering of the reality behind the illusions and ideologies
which cover it. In this lies the reason for a unique feature
of Marxist propaganda: it is an emotional appeal for certain political aims, blended with a scientific analysis of
social and historical phenomena. The best known example
for this blend is, of course, the Communist Manifesto. This
contains in a brief form a brilliant and lucid analysis of
history, of the influence of economic factors, of class relations. And at the same time it is a political pamphlet ending with a fervently emotional appeal to the working class.
The fact that the political leader must be at the same time
a social scientist and a writer was demonstrated not only

by Marx. Engels, Bebel, Jaurés, Rosa Luxemburg, Lenin and many other leaders of the socialist movement were writers and students of social science and politics. (Even Stalin, a man with little literary or scientific talent, was forced to write books or to have them written in his name in order to prove his legitimacy as Marx's and Lenin's successor.) In fact, however, under Stalin this aspect of socialism completely changed. Since the Soviet system must not be the subject matter of scientific analysis, the Soviet social scientists have become apologists for their system and have a scientific function only in technical matters dealing with production, distribution, organization, etc.

While for Marx truth was a weapon to induce social change, for Freud it was the weapon to induce individual change; *awareness* was the main agent in Freud's therapy. If, so Freud found, the patient can gain insight into the fictitious character of his conscious ideas, if he can grasp the reality behind these ideas, if he can make the unconscious conscious, he will attain the strength to rid himself of his irrationalities and to transform himself. Freud's aim, "Where there is Id there shall be Ego," can be realized only through the effort of reason to penetrate fictions and to arrive at the awareness of reality. It is precisely this function of reason and truth which gives psychoanalytic therapy its unique feature among all forms of therapy. Each analysis of a patient is a new and original venture of research. While it is true, of course, that there are general theories and principles which can be applied, there is no pattern, no "formula" which could be applied to the individual patient or be helpful to him if it were applied. Just as for Marx the political leader must be a social scientist, so for Freud the therapist must be a scientist capable of doing research. For both, truth is the essential medium to transform, respectively, society and the individual; awareness is the key to social and individual therapy.

Marx's statement, "The demand to give up the illusions about its condition is the demand to give up a condition which needs illusions," also could have been made by Freud. Both wanted to free man from the chains of his illusions in order to enable him to wake up and to act as a free man.

The third basic element common to both systems is their humanism. Humanism in the sense that each man represents all of humanity; hence, that there is nothing human which could be alien to him. Marx was rooted in this tradition, of which Voltaire, Lessing, Herder, Hegel, and Goethe are some of the most outstanding representatives. Freud expressed his humanism primarily in his concept of the unconscious. He assumed that all men share the same unconscious strivings, and hence that they can understand each other once they dare to delve into the underworld of the unconscious. He could examine the unconscious fantasies of his patient without feeling indignant, judgmental, or even surprised. The "stuff from which dreams are made" as well as the whole world of the unconscious became an object of investigation precisely because Freud recognized its profoundly human and universal qualities.

Doubt and the power of truth and humanism are the guiding and propelling principles of Marx's and Freud's work. Yet this introductory chapter that deals with the common soil from which both their ideas grew, would be truncated if it did not deal at least with one other feature common to both systems: their dynamic and dialectic approach to reality. The discussion of this topic is all the more important because in the Anglo-Saxon countries Hegelian philosophy has been a dead issue for a long time so that the dynamic approach of Marx and Freud

is not readily understood. Let us begin with a few examples, both from the realm of psychology and that of
sociology.

Let us assume a man who has been married three
times. The pattern is always the same. He falls in love with
a good looking girl, marries her, and is ecstatically happy
for a short time. Then he begins to complain that his wife
is domineering, that she curtails his freedom, etc. After
a period alternating between quarrels and reconciliations,
he falls in love with another girl—in fact, one very similar
to his wife. He gets a divorce and marries his second
"great love." However, with slight modifications the same
cycle takes place, and again he falls in love with a similar
type of girl, and again he gets divorced and marries his
third "great love." Again the same cycle occurs, and he
falls in love with a fourth girl, being convinced that this
time it is the true and real love (forgetting that he was
convinced of that every time in the past), and wants
to marry her. What would we say to the last girl if she
asked us our opinion about the chances for a happy
marriage with him? There are several approaches to the
problem. The first one is a purely behavioristic one; the
method of this approach is to conclude from past behavior, the future behavior. This argument would run:
since he already has left a wife three times, it is quite likely
that he will do it a fourth time, hence it is much too
risky to marry him. This approach, empirical and sober,
has much to be said for it. But the girl's mother, when using
this approach, might find it difficult to answer one argument of her daughter's. This argument says that while it
is perfectly true that he did act in the same way three
times, it does not follow that he will do so again this
time. Either, so this counter-argument will say, he has
changed—and who can say that a person may not change?
Or the other women were not really the kind he could

love deeply, while she, the last one, is really congenial to him. There is no convincing argument the mother could use against this reasoning. In fact, once she sees the man and notices that he is very much enraptured with her daughter, and that he talks with great sincerity about his love, even the mother might change her mind and be won over to the daughter's position.

The mother's and the daughter's approaches are both undynamic. They either make a prediction based on past performance, or one based on present words and actions, yet they have no way of proving that their predictions are better than guesswork.

What is, in contradistinction, the dynamic approach? The essential point in this approach is to penetrate through the surface of past or present behavior and to understand the *forces* which created the pattern of past behavior. If these forces still exist, it is to be assumed that the fourth marriage will end not differently from the previous ones. If, on the other hand, there has been a change in the forces underlying his behavior, one would have to admit the possibility or even the likelihood of a different outcome, in spite of the past behavior. What are the forces we speak of here? They are nothing mysterious, nor figments of abstract speculation. They are recognizable empirically if one studies the behavior of the person in the proper way. We may assume, for instance, that the man had not cut the tie to his mother; that he is a very narcissistic person with a deep doubt of his own manliness; that he is an overgrown adolescent in constant need of admiration and affection, so that once he has found a woman who fulfills these needs he gets bored with her soon after the conquest is made; he needs new proofs of his attractiveness and hence must look for another woman who can reassure him. At the same time he is really dependent on women, afraid of them; and hence any prolonged intimacy makes him feel imprisoned and chained. The forces at work here are his narcissism, his dependence, his self-doubt producing needs which lead to the kind of action we have been describing. These forces, as I said, are by no means the result of abstract speculation. One can observe them in many ways: by examining dreams, free association, fantasies, by watching his facial expression, his gestures, his way of speaking, and so forth. Yet they are often not directly visible but must be inferred. Furthermore, they can be seen only within the theoretical frame of reference in which they have a place and meaning. Most importantly, these forces are not only not conscious as such, but they are in contradiction to the conscious thought of the person involved. He is sincerely convinced that he will love the girl forever, that he is not dependent, that he is strong and self-assured. Thus, the average person thinks: if a man truly feels he loves a woman how can one predict that he will leave her after a short time, just by referring to such mythical entities as "fixation to mother," "narcissism," and so on? Are one's eyes and ears not better judges than such deductions?

The problem in Marxian sociology is precisely the same. An example also will be the best introduction here. Germany has started two wars, one in 1914 and one in 1939, in which she almost succeeded in conquering her Western neighbors and in defeating Russia. After an initial success, Germany was defeated both times largely by the overwhelming power of the United States; Germany's economy was badly damaged, yet both times there was a quick recovery, and five to ten years after the war the country had achieved an economic and military power similar to the one it possessed before the war. Today, a little over fifteen years after a defeat which was much more crushing than that suffered in the war of 1914–18, Germany is again the strongest industrial and military power (after the Soviet Union) in Europe. She has lost a considerable part of her former territory, yet is more prosperous than ever before. The present-day Germany has a democratic regime; it has a small army, navy, and air force; it declares that it will not try to reconquer the lost territories by force although it has not given up the claims to these territories. This new Germany is looked upon with suspicion and dread by the Soviet states and by small groups in Western countries. The reasoning in these circles is that Germany has attacked her neighbors twice, has rearmed in spite of two defeats, that the generals of the "new" Germany are the same generals who served Hitler, and that it is to be expected that Germany will make a third try and this time attack the Soviet Union in order to recover her lost territories. To this argument the leaders of the NATO countries and the majority of public opinion answer that these suspicions are unwarranted and, in fact, quite fantastic: is this not a new and democratic Germany, have its leaders not declared that they want peace, is the German army not so small (twelve divisions) that it cannot be a menace to anybody? If one looks only at the utterances of the German government (even believing that they speak the truth) and at the present German strength, then indeed, the NATO position seems quite convincing. If one argues that the Germans will attack again because they have done it before, one has also a rather good argument, except that one does not disprove that Germany may have completely changed. Here, as in the psychological example above, one leaves the realm of guessing only if one begins to analyze the forces behind the German development.

Germany, the latecomer among the great Western industrial systems, began its spectacular rise after 1871. In 1895 her steel production already had reached the level of Great Britain's; and by 1914 Germany was far ahead of England and of France. Germany had a most efficient industrial machine (greatly supported by a sober, industrious, educated, working class) but not enough raw materials, and few colonies. In order to realize her economic potential maximally, she had to expand, to conquer territories that had raw materials in Europe and in Africa. At the same time the Prussian tradition had provided Germany with an officer's caste with a long tradition of discipline, loyalty, and devotion to the army. The industrial potential with its inherent tendency for expansion, blended with the ability and ambition of the military caste, was the explosive mixture which led Germany on her first war adventure in 1914. While the German government under Bethmann-Hollweg did not seek war, it was pushed into it by the military men, and already three months after the beginning of the war it accepted the war aims presented to the government by the representatives of the German heavy industry and the big banks. These war aims were more or less the same as those demanded by the *Alldeutscher Verband,* the political spearhead of these industrial circles since the nineties: French, Belgian, and Luxembourg coal and iron resources, colonies in Africa (especially Katanga), and some territories in the East. Germany lost the war, but the same industrialists and officers retained their power, in spite of the revolution which seemed to threaten that power for a short while. In the thirties, Germany had achieved again the superior status it held before 1914. But the great economic crisis with six millions of unemployed threatened the whole capitalistic system. Both socialists and communists were not too far from having one half of the popular votes, and in addition the Nazis rallied millions under their allegedly anticapitalist platform. The industrialists, bankers, and generals accepted Hitler's offer to smash the parties of the left and the trade unions and to build up a nationalist spirit together with a new and strong army. In return he was permitted to execute his racial program, a program which his industrial and military allies did not like particularly, but to which they did not object too much either. The only Nazi force which could have been a threat to the industrialists and to the army, the S.A. troops, was destroyed by the wholesale murder of its leaders in 1934. Hitler's aim was the execution of the same program which had been Ludendorf's in 1914. This time the generals were more reluctant in planning the war. But being supported by the sympathies of the Western governments, Hitler was able to convince his generals of his superior talent and of the correctness of his military plans. He won their support for the war of 1939 which had the same aims as had been the Kaiser's in 1914. While the West was sympathetic to Hitler until 1938 and hardly protested against his racial and political persecutions, the situation changed when he ceased to proceed with caution and thus forced Great Britain and France into a war. From then on it was made to appear that the war against Hitler was a war against dictatorship, while it was, like the war of 1914, a war against an attack on the economic and political position of the Western powers.

After the defeat, Germany made use of the legend that the Second World War had been a war against Nazi dictatorship by ridding itself of the most obvious and best-known Nazi leaders (and by paying considerable sums to the Jews and the Israeli government, as reparations), and by thus claiming that the new Germany was entirely different from that of the Kaiser or that of Hitler. But in reality the basic situation had not altered. The German industry is as strong today as it was before the Second World War, except that the territory has shrunk still more. The German military class is still the same, even though the Junkers have lost their economic bases in East Prussia.

The forces of German expansionism which existed in 1914 and in 1939 are still the same, this time provided with a more powerful charge of emotional dynamism: the clamor for the return of the "stolen" territories. The German leaders have learned; this time they start out with an alliance with the United States, instead of having the strongest Western power as a potential enemy. This time they have joined in a merger with all of Western Europe with a good chance of emerging as the leading power of the new Federated Europe, being already the strongest power, economically and militarily. The New Europe, led by Germany, will be as expansionist as the Old Germany was; eager to recover the former German territories, it will be an even greater menace to peace. By this I do not imply that Germany wants war, and certainly not thermonuclear war. What I mean to say is that the New Germany hopes to attain its aims without war, by the very threat of an overwhelming force once this has been attained.[1] But this calculation is most likely to lead to war, since the Soviet bloc will not stand by quietly while Germany gets stronger and stronger—just as little as Great Britain and France did in 1914 and in 1939.

Again the point here is that there are economic, social, and emotional forces at work which have produced two wars within twenty-five years, and which are likely to produce another one. Not that anyone *wants* war; these forces operate behind people's backs and lead to certain developments which produce war. Only an analysis of these forces can help us to understand the past and to predict

---

[1] Adenauer, in a Radio interview on March 6, 1952 stated: "Once the West is strong, there will be a real starting point for peaceful negotiations with the goal to liberate in peace not only the Soviet Zone but the whole of the enslaved Europe east of the Iron Curtain."

the future—not a view which is restricted to the observation of phenomena as they exist at the moment.

Marx had forerunners as well as Freud. Yet each of them for the first time approached his subject matter in a spirit of scientific understanding. They did for society and for the individual respectively what physiology did for the living cell and theoretical physics for the atom. Marx saw society as an intricate structure with various contradictory yet ascertainable forces. The knowledge of these forces permits the understanding of the past and to some extent the prediction of the future—prediction not in the sense of events which will necessarily occur, but rather of limited alternatives between which man has to choose.

Freud discovered that man as a mental entity is a structure of forces, many of them contradictory, charged with energy. Here too, what matters is the scientific task of understanding the quality, intensity, and direction of these forces in order to understand the past and predict alternatives for the future. Here too, change is possible only inasmuch as the given structure of the forces permits it. Furthermore, true change in the sense of energy changes within the given structure does not only require a profound understanding of these forces and the laws according to which they move but also great effort and will.

The common soil from which both Marx's and Freud's thought grew is, in the last analysis, the concept of humanism and humanity which, going back to the Judaeo-Christian and Greco-Roman tradition, made its new entry into European history with the Renaissance and unfolded fully in the eighteenth and nineteenth centuries. The humanistic ideal of the Renaissance was the unfolding of the total, universal man (*uomo universale*) who was considered to be the highest flowering of natural development.

Freud's defense of the rights of man's natural drives against the forces of social convention, as well as his ideal that reason controls and ennobles these drives, is part of the tradition of humanism. Marx's protest against a social order in which man is crippled by his subservience to the economy, and his ideal of the full unfolding of the total, unalienated man, is part of the same humanistic tradition. Freud's vision was narrowed down by his mechanistic, materialistic philosophy which interpreted the needs of human nature as being essentially sexual ones. Marx's vision was a much wider one precisely because he saw the crippling effect of class society, and thus could have a vision of the uncrippled man and the possibilities for his development, once society had become entirely human. Freud was a liberal reformer; Marx, a radical revolutionist. Different as they were, they have in common an uncompromising will to liberate man, an equally uncompromising faith in truth as the instrument of liberation and the belief that the condition for this liberation lies in man's capacity to break the chain of illusion.

III

THE CONCEPT OF MAN
AND HIS NATURE

THAT ALL men share the same basic anatomical and physiological features is common knowledge, and no physician would think he could not treat every man, regardless of race and color, with the same methods he has applied to men of his own race. But does man have also in common the same psychic organization; do all men have in common the same human nature? Is there such an entity as "human nature?"

This question is by no means of a purely academic nature. If men differed in their basic psychic and mental structure, how could we speak of humanity in more than a physiological and anatomical sense? How could we understand the "stranger" if he were fundamentally different from us? How could we understand the art of entirely different cultures, their myths, their drama, their sculpture, were it not for the fact that we all share the same human nature?

The whole concept of humanity and of humanism is based on the idea of a human nature in which all men share. This was the premise of Buddhist as well as of Judæo-Christian thought. The former developed a picture of man in existentialist and anthropological terms and assumed that the same psychic laws are valid for all men

27

because the "human situation" is the same for all of us; that we all live under the illusion of the separateness and indestructibility of each one's ego; that we all try to find an answer to the problem of existence by the greedy desire to hold on to things, including that peculiar thing, "I"; that we all suffer because this answer to life is a false one, and that we can get rid of the suffering only by giving the right answer—that of overcoming the illusion of separateness, of overcoming greed, and of waking up to the fundamental truths which govern our existence.

The Judæo-Christian tradition, being conceptualized in reference to a supreme creator and ruler, God, defined man in a different way. One man and one woman are the forebears of the whole human race, and these forebears as well as all the generations to come are made in "the likeness of God." They all share the same basic features that make them human, which enable them to know and to love one another. This is the premise for the prophetic picture of the Messianic Time, the peaceful unity of all mankind.

Among the philosophers, Spinoza, the father of modern dynamic psychology, postulated the picture of the nature of man in terms of a "model of human nature," which was ascertainable and definable and from which the laws of human behavior and reaction followed. Man, and not just men of this or of that culture, could be understood like any other being in nature because man is one, and the same laws are valid for all of us at all times. The philosophers of the eighteenth and nineteenth centuries (especially Goethe and Herder) believed that the humanity (*Humanitaet*) inherent in man leads him to ever higher stages of development; they believed that every individual carries within himself not only his individuality but also all of humanity with all its potentialities. They considered the task of life to be the development toward totality through individuality; and they believed that the voice of humanity was given to everybody and could be understood by every human being.[1]

Today the idea of a human nature or of an essence of man has fallen into disrepute, partly because one has become more skeptical about metaphysical and abstract terms like "the essence of man," but partly also because one has lost the experience of humanity which underlay the Buddhist, Judæo-Christian, Spinozist, and Enlightenment concepts. Contemporary psychologists and sociologists are prone to think of man as a blank sheet of paper on which each culture writes its text. While they do not deny the oneness of the human race, they leave hardly any content and substance to this concept of humanity.

In contrast to these contemporary trends, Marx and Freud assumed that man's behavior is comprehensible precisely because it is the behavior of *man,* of a species that can be defined in terms of its psychic and mental character.

Marx, in assuming the existence of a nature of man, did not concur in the common error of confusing it with its particular manifestations. He differentiated "human nature in general" from "human nature as modified in each historical epoch."[2] Human nature in general we can never see, of course, as such, because what we observe are always the specific manifestations of human nature in various cultures. But we can infer from these various manifestations

---

[1] Cf. H. A. Korff, *Geist der Goethezeit* (Leipzig: Koehler and Amelang, 1958, 4th edition), and the brilliant paper on Goethe's *Iphigenia and the Humane Ideal,* Oscar Seidline, *Essays in German Comparative Literature* (Chapel Hill, N. C.: University of North Carolina Press, 1961)

[2] Karl Marx, *Capital I* (Chicago: Charles H. Kerr Co., 1906), p. 668.

what this "human nature in general" is, what the laws are
which govern it, what the needs are which man has as man.

In his earlier writings Marx still called "human nature
in general" the "essence of man." He later gave up this
term because he wanted to make it clear that "the essence
of man is no *abstraction* inherent in each separate individual." [1,2] Marx also wanted to avoid giving the impression that he thought of the essence of man as an
unhistorical substance. For Marx, the nature of man was
a given potential, a set of conditions, the human raw
material, as it were, which as such cannot be changed, just
as the size and structure of the human brain has remained
the same since the beginning of civilization. Yet man
does change in the course of history. He is the product
of history, transforming himself during his history. He becomes what he potentially is. History is the process of
man's creating himself by developing—in the process of
work—those potentialities which are given him when he
is born. *"The whole of what is called world history,"* says
Marx, "is nothing but the creation of man by human labor, and the emergence of nature for man; he therefore

---

[1] K. Marx and F. Engels, *German Ideology,* edited with an introduction by R. Pascal (New York: International Publishers Co.,
Inc., 1939), p. 198. (My italics, E.F.)

[2] It has been said by representatives of Soviet Marxism and by
some noncommunist writers that the views of the "young Marx"
as expressed in the Philosophical Manuscripts are fundamentally
different from those of the "mature Marx." I believe, however,
with most non-Soviet Marxists and socialist humanists that this
interpretation is untenable and serves only the purpose of identify-
ing Soviet ideology with Marx's ideas. Cf. the discussion of this
point in E. Fromm, *Marx's Concept of Man* (New York:
Frederick Ungar Publishing Co., Inc., 1961), p. 69 ff. and Robert
Tucker, *Philosophy and Myth in Karl Marx* (Cambridge University Press, 1961).

has the evident and irrefutable proof of his *self-creation* of his own *origins.*" [1]

Marx was opposed to two positions: the unhistorical one that the nature of man is a substance present from the very beginning of history, and the relativistic position that man's nature has no inherent quality whatsoever and is nothing but the reflex of social conditions. But he never arrived at the full development of his own theory concerning the nature of man, transcending both the unhistorical and the relativistic positions; hence he left himself open to various and contradictory interpretations.

Nevertheless from his concept of man follow certain ideas about human pathology and about human health. As the main manifestation of psychic pathology, Marx speaks of the *crippled* and of the *alienated* man; as the main manifestation of psychic health, he speaks of the active, productive, independent man. To these concepts we shall return later, after having discussed the concept of human motivation in Marx and in Freud.

At this point, however, we must return first to the concept of human nature in *Freud's* thinking. It hardly needs to be explained to anybody familiar with Freud's system that the subject matter of his investigation was man *qua* man or, to speak with Spinoza, that Freud constructed a "model of human nature." This model was constructed in the spirit of nineteenth-century materialistic thought. Man is conceived as a machine, driven by a relatively constant amount of sexual energy called "libido." This libido causes painful tension, which is reduced only by the act of physi-

---

[1] K. Marx, *Economic and Philosophical Manuscripts,* translated by T. B. Bottomore in E. Fromm's *Marx's Concept of Man,* p. 139. In the following pages, the quotations from the Economic and Philosophical Manuscripts refer to this publication in *Marx's Concept of Man,* with the corresponding pagination.

cal release; to this liberation from painful tension Freud gave the name of "pleasure." After the reduction of tension, libidinal tension increases again due to the chemistry of the body, causing a new need for tension reduction, that is, pleasureful satisfaction. This dynamism, which leads from tension to release of tension to renewed tension, from pain to pleasure to pain, Freud called the "pleasure principle." He contrasted it with the "reality principle," which tells man what to seek for and what to avoid in the real world in which he lives, in order to secure his survival. This reality principle often conflicts with the pleasure principle, and a certain equilibrium between the two is the condition for mental health. On the other hand, if either one of these two principles is out of balance, neurotic or psychotic manifestations are the result.

IV

HUMAN EVOLUTION

F<small>REUD</small>, like Marx, sees the development of man in evolutionary terms. In his ideas about the *development of the individual,* Freud assumes that the main driving force, sexual energy, itself undergoes an evolution which occurs from birth to puberty in the life of each individual. The libido goes through certain stages: first it is centered around the sucking and biting activities of the infant, then around the process of anal and urethral elimination, eventually around the genital apparatus. The libido is the same and yet not the same in the history of each individual; its potential is the same, but its manifestations change in the process of individual evolution.

Freud's picture of the *development of the human race* resembles in some aspects that of individual development, while it differs in others. He sees primitive man as one who gives full satisfaction to all his instincts, and also to those perverse instincts which are part of primitive sexuality. But this primitive man, fully satisfied instinctually, is not a creator of culture and civilization. Yet man, for reasons which Freud fails to elucidate, begins to create civilization. This very creation of his forces him to forego the immediate and complete satisfaction of his instincts; the frustrated instinct is turned into nonsexual mental and psychic energy, which is the building stone for civilization. (Freud called this transformation from sexual to nonsexual energy "sublimation," using an analogy from chemistry.) The more civilization grows, the more man sublimates, but the more he also frustrates his original libidinous impulses. He becomes wiser and more cultured, but he is also in some sense less happy than primitive man was and increasingly more prone to neuroses, which are the result of too much instinctual frustration. Thus man becomes discontented with the very civilization he creates. While historical development is a positive phenomenon, if seen from the standpoint of the products of civilization, it is also a development which implies increasing discontent and increasing possibilities for neurosis.

Another aspect of Freud's historical theory is connected with the "Oedipus complex." In *Totem and Taboo* he develops the hypothesis that the decisive step from primitive to civilized history lies in the rebellion of the sons against the father, and the murder of the hated father. The sons then create a system of society based on a covenant which excludes further murder among the rivals and provides for the establishment of morality. The evolution of the child, according to Freud, follows a similar path. The little boy at the age of five or six is intensely jealous of his father and represses murderous wishes against him only under the pressure of the castration threat. In order to liberate himself from continuous fear, he internalizes the incest taboo, and thus builds the nucleus around which his "conscience" is to grow (superego). Later on, the prohibitions and commands voiced by other authorities and by society are added to the original taboos voiced by father.

Marx did not attempt to outline a sketch of individual evolution. He was concerned only with the development of man in history.

History, according to Marx, is determined in its course

by continuous contradictions. The productive forces grow and thus conflict with the older economic, social, and political forms. This conflict (for instance, between the steam engine and the previous social organization of manufacturing) leads to social and economic changes. The new stability, however, again is challenged by further development of the productive forces (for instance, from the steam engine to the use of gasoline, electricity, atomic energy), leading to new social forms which correspond better to the new productive forces. Together with the conflict between productive forces and socio-political structures goes the conflict between social classes. The feudal class based on older forms of production is in conflict with the new middle class of small manufacturers and businessmen; this middle class finds itself fighting, at some later point, against the working class as well as the leaders of big monopolistic enterprises which tend to strangle the earlier and smaller forms of enterprise.

Man's psychic evolution takes place within the historical process. The central concept in Marx's evolutionary theory lies in man's relationship to nature, and in the development of this relationship. In the beginning of history he is completely dependent on nature. In the process of evolution he makes himself more and more independent of nature, begins to rule and transform nature in the process of work, and in transforming nature man transforms himself. Man's dependence on nature limits his freedom and his capacity for thought; he is in many ways like a child. He slowly grows up, and only when he has fully mastered nature and thus become an independent being can he develop all his intellectual and emotional faculties. For Marx, a socialist society is the one in which the grownup man begins to unfold all his powers. The following paragraph, taken from *Capital*, expresses some of Marx's ideas on this subject: "Those ancient social organisms of production are, as com-

pared with bourgeois society, extremely simple and trans-
parent. But they are founded either on the immature development of man individually, *who has not yet severed the
umbilical cord that unites him with his fellow man in a
primitive tribal community,* or upon direct relations of
subjection. They can arise and exist only when the development of the productive power of labor has not risen beyond a low state, and when, therefore, the social relations
within the sphere of material life, between man and man,
and between man and nature, are correspondingly narrow.
This narrowness is reflected in the ancient worship of Nature, and in the other elements of the popular religions.
The religious reflex of the real world can, in any case, only
then finally vanish when the practical relations of every-
day life offer to man none but perfectly intelligible and
reasonable relations with regard to his fellow men and to
nature. The life-process of material production does not
strip off its mystical veil until it is treated as production by
freely associated men, and is consciously regulated by them
in accordance with a settled plan. This, however, demands
for society a certain material groundwork or set of conditions of existence which in their turn are the spontaneous
product of a long and painful process of development." [1]

Man, as a race, slowly emancipates himself from mother
nature through the process of work, and in this process of
emancipation he develops his intellectual and emotional
powers and grows up, becomes an independent and free
man. When he will have brought nature under his full and
rational control, and when society will have lost its an-
tagonistic class character, "prehistory" will have ended,
and a truly human history will begin in which free men
plan and organize their exchange with nature, and in which
the aim and end of all social life is not work and produc-

---

[1] *Capital* I., pp. 91-2 (My italics, E.F.).

tion, but the unfolding of man's powers as an end in itself. This is, for Marx, the realm of freedom in which man will be fully united with his fellow men and with nature.

The contrast between Marx and Freud with regard to history is quite clear. Marx had an unbroken faith in man's perfectibility and progress, rooted in the Messianic tradition of the West from the prophets through Christianity, the Renaissance, and Enlightenment thinking. Freud, especially the Freud after the First World War, was a skeptic. He saw the problem of human evolution as an essentially tragic one. Whatever man did, it ended in frustration; if he should return to become a primitive again, he would have pleasure, but no wisdom; if he goes on as a builder of ever more complicated civilizations, he becomes wiser, but also unhappier and sicker. For Freud, evolution is an ambiguous blessing, and society does as much harm as it does good. For Marx, history is a march toward man's self-realization; society, whatever the evils produced by any given society may be, is the condition for man's self-creation and unfolding. The "good society" for Marx becomes identical with the society of good men, that is, of fully developed, sane, and productive individuals.

V

HUMAN MOTIVATION

W<small>HAT</small> are the motivating forces which make man act in certain ways, the drives which propel him to strive in certain directions?

It seems as if in the answer to this question Marx and Freud find themselves furthest apart and that there is an insoluble contradiction between their two systems. Marx's "materialistic" theory of history is usually understood to mean that man's main motivation is his wish for material satisfaction, his desire to use and to have more and more. This greed for material things as man's essential motivation is then contrasted with Freud's concept according to which it is man's sexual appetite which constitutes his most potent motivation for action. The desire for property on the one hand and the desire for sexual satisfaction on the other seem to be the two conflicting theories as far as human motivation is concerned.

That this assumption is an oversimplifying distortion as far as Freud is concerned follows from what has been already said about this theory. Freud sees man as motivated by contradictions; by the contradiction between his striving for sexual pleasure and his striving for survival and mastery of his environment. This conflict became even more complicated when Freud later posited another factor which

38

conflicted with the ones already mentioned—the super-ego, the incorporated authority of the father and the norms he represented. For Freud, then, man is motivated by forces conflicting with each other and by no means only by the desire for sexual satisfaction.[1]

The cliché of Marx's theory of motivation is an even more drastic distortion of his thinking than the cliché of Freud's. The distortion begins with the misunderstanding of the term "materialism." This term and its counterpart, "idealism," have two entirely different meanings, depending on the context in which they are applied. When applied to human attitudes, one refers to the "materialist" as one who is mainly concerned with the satisfaction of material strivings, and to the "idealist" as one who is motivated by an idea, that is, a spiritual or ethical motivation. But "materialism" and "idealism" have entirely different meanings in philosophical terminology, and "materialism" must be used in this meaning when one refers to Marx's "historical materialism" (a term which, in fact, Marx himself never used). Philosophically, idealism means that one assumes ideas form the basic reality, and that the material world which we perceive by means of our senses has no reality as such. For the materialism prevalent at the end of the nineteenth century matter was real, not ideas. Marx, in contrast to this mechanical materialism (which was also underlying Freud's thinking), was not concerned with the causal relationship between matter and mind but with understanding all phenomena as results of the *activity of real human beings*. "In direct contrast to German philosophy," Marx wrote, "which descends from the heaven to earth, here we ascend from earth to heaven. That is to say, we

---

[1] In a further development of his theories, which I mention only in passing, Freud again thought in terms of a contradiction, that between the "life instinct" and the "death instinct" as the two forces battling constantly within man and motivating his actions.

do not set out from what men imagine, conceive, in order to arrive at man in the flesh. *We set out from real active men and on the basis of their real life process we demonstrate the development of the ideological reflexes and echoes of this life process."* [1]

Marx's "materialism" implies that we begin our study of man with the real man as we find him, and not with his ideas about himself and the world by which he tries to explain himself. In order to understand how this confusion between personal and philosophical materialism could have arisen in the case of Marx, we must proceed further and consider Marx's so-called "economic theory of history." This term has been misunderstood to mean that, according to Marx, only economic motives determine man's actions in the historical process; in other words, the "economic" factor has been understood to refer to a psychological, subjective motive, that of economic interests. But Marx never meant this. Historical materialism is not at all a *psychological* theory; its main postulate is that the way in which man produces determines his practice of life, his way of living, and this practice of life determines his thinking and the social and political structure of his society. Economy in this context refers *not to a psychic drive, but to the mode of production;* not to a *subjective psychological* but to an *objective socio-economic* factor. Marx's idea that man is formed by his practice of life was not new as such. Montesquieu had expressed the same idea in terms of "institutions form men"; Robert Owen expressed it in similar ways. What was new in Marx's system is that he analyzed in detail what these institutions are, or rather, that the institutions themselves were to be understood as part of the whole system of production which characterizes a given society. Various economic conditions can pro-

---

[1] *German Ideology,* p. 14. (My italics, E.F.)

duce different psychological motivations. One economic system may lead to the formation of ascetic tendencies, as early capitalism did; another economic system to the preponderance of the desire to save and hoard, as nineteenth century capitalism did; still another, to the preponderance of the desire for spending and for ever-increasing consumption, as twentieth century capitalism does. There is only one quasi-psychological premise in Marx's system: man must first of all eat and drink, have shelter and clothing, before he can pursue politics, science, art, religion, etc. Therefore the production of the immediate material means of subsistence, and consequently the degree of economic development attained by a given society, form the foundation upon which social and political institutions, and even art and religion, have been evolved. Man himself, in each period of history, is formed in terms of the prevailing practice of life which in turn is determined by his mode of production. All this does not mean, however, that the drive to produce or consume is man's main motivation. On the contrary, Marx's main criticism of capitalist society is precisely that this society makes the wish to "have" and to "use" into the most dominant desire in man; Marx believed that a man who is dominated by the desire to have and to use is a crippled man. His aim was a socialist society organized in such a way that *not* profit and private property, but the free unfolding of man's human powers are man's dominant aims. Not the man who *has* much, but the man who *is* much is the fully developed, truly human man.

It is indeed one of the most drastic examples of man's capacity for distortion and rationalization that Marx is attacked by the spokesmen for capitalism because of his allegedly "materialistic" aims. Not only is this not true, but what is paradoxical is that the same spokesmen for capitalism combat socialism by saying that the profit motive— on which capitalism is based—is the only potent motive for human creative activity, and that socialism could not work effectively because it excludes the profit motive as the main stimulus in the economy. All this is even more complex and paradoxical if one considers that Russian communism has adopted this capitalist thinking, and that for Soviet managers, workers, and peasants, the profit motive is by far the most important incentive in the present Soviet economy. Not only in practice but often also in theoretical statements about human motivation, the Soviet system and the capitalist system agree with each other, and both are equally in contradiction to Marx's theories and aims.[1]

---

[1] Tucker wrongly assumes that Marx believed that the compulsion that transforms free creative self-activity into alienated labour is the compulsion to amass wealth. Tucker's error is based on an erroneous translation of the Marx text he refers to. Marx says, in the *Economic and Philosophical Manuscripts:* "die einzigen Raeder, die die National Oekonomie in Bewegung *setzt,* sind die Habsucht," etc. This means: "the only wheels that political economy *sets* in motion are greed," and not as Tucker translates, "the only wheels that *set* political economy in motion are greed." Subject and predicate are reversed.

VI

THE SICK INDIVIDUAL
AND THE SICK SOCIETY

W<small>HAT</small> is the concept of psychic pathology in Freud and in Marx? Freud's concept is well-known. It assumes that if man fails to solve his Oedipus complex, or to put it differently, if man does not overcome his infantile strivings and develop a mature genital orientation, he is torn between the desires of the child within himself and the claims which he makes as a grown-up person. The neurotic symptom represents a compromise between infantile and grown-up needs, while the psychosis is that form of pathology in which the infantile desires and phantasies have flooded the grown-up ego, and thus there is no more compromise between the two worlds.

Marx, of course, never developed a systematic psychopathology, yet he speaks of one form of psychic crippledness which to him is the most fundamental expression of psychopathology and which to overcome is the goal of socialism: *alienation.*[1]

---

[1] The concept of alienation has become increasingly the focus of the discussion of Marx's ideas in England, France, Germany, and the U.S.A., as well as in Yugoslavia and Poland. The majority of those involved in this debate which includes Protestant and Catholic theologians, as well as humanist socialists take a

What does Marx mean by alienation (or "estrangement")? The essence of this concept, which was first developed by Hegel, is that the world (nature, things, others, and he himself) have become alien to man. He does not experience himself as the subject of his own acts, as a thinking, feeling, loving person, but he experiences himself only in the things he has created, as the object of the externalized manifestations of his powers. He is in touch with himself only by surrendering himself to the products of his creation.

Hegel, taking God as the subject of history, had seen God in man, in a state of self-alienation and in the process of history God's return to himself.

Feuerbach turned Hegel upside down; [1] God, so he thought, represented man's own powers transferred from man, the owner of these powers, to a being outside of him, so that man is in touch with his own powers only by his worship of God; the stronger and richer God is, the weaker and poorer becomes man.

Marx was deeply stirred and influenced by Feuerbach's thought. In his introduction to the Critique of Hegel's Philosophy of Right (written toward the end of 1843) he followed Feuerbach in his analysis of alienation. In his Economic-Philosophical Manuscripts (1844) Marx pro-

---

position that alienation and the task of overcoming it is the center of Marx's socialist humanism and the aim of socialism; furthermore that there is a complete continuity between the young and the mature Marx, in spite of changes in terminology and emphasis (to this group belong, to mention only a few, Rubel, Goldman, Bottomore, Fromm, Petrovic, Markovic, Vranicki, Bloch, Lukacs.) Other authors like D. Bell, L. Feuer, and to some extent C. W. Mills have taken the position that alienation is either not a useful, or a central theme in Marx.

[1] Cf. the discussion on alienation in R. Tucker's *Philosophy and Myth in Karl Marx*. Cambridge University Press, 1961, pp. 85 ff.

ceeded from the phenomenon of *religious alienation* to that of the *alienation of labor*. Parallel to Feuerbach's analysis of religious alienation Marx wrote: "The worker becomes poorer, the more wealth he produces and the more his production increases in power and extent." [1] And a few paragraphs later he wrote: "All these consequences follow from the fact that the worker is related to the *product of his labor* as to an *alien* object. For it is clear on this presupposition that the more the worker expends himself in work, the more powerful becomes the world of objects which he creates in face of himself, the poorer he becomes in his inner life and the less he belongs to himself; it is just the same as in religion. The more of himself man attributes to God the less he has left in himself. The worker puts his life into the object and his life then belongs no longer to himself but to the object. The greater his activity, therefore, the less he possess . . . The *alienation* of the worker in his product means not only that his labor becomes an object, assumes an external existence, but that it exists independently, outside himself that it stands opposed to him as an autonomous power. The life which he has given to the object sets itself against him as an alien and hostile force." [2] But, so Marx goes on to say, the worker is not only alienated from the products which he creates; "alienation appears not only in the result, but also in the *process,* of production, within *productive activity* itself." [3] And again he returns to the analogy of aliena-

---

[1] *Economic and Philosophical Manuscripts,* p. 95. It may not be too farfetched to speculate that Marx was influenced in his erroneous theory of the increasing impoverishment of the worker in the process of capitalistic evolution by this analogy between religious and economic alienation even though his economic assumption *seems* to be nothing but the logical outcome of his economic theory of labor, value, and other factors.

[2] *Ibid.,* pp. 95-6.

[3] *Ibid., p.* 99.

tion in labor with alienation in religion, "Just as in religion the spontaneous activity 'Selbsttaetigkeit' of human fantasy, of the human brain and heart, reacts independently as an alien activity of gods and devils upon the individual, so the activity of the worker is not his own spontaneous activity." [1]

From the concept of alienated work, Marx proceeds to the concept of man's alienation from himself, his fellowman, and from nature. He defines labor in its original and nonalienated form as "life activity, productive life "Lebenstaetigkeit, das produktiv Leben"," and then proceeds to define the species character of man as "free, conscious activity." ('freie bewusste Taetigkeit') In alienated labor the free and conscious activity of man becomes distorted into alienated activity and thus "Life itself appears only as a *means of life.*" [2]

As the previous statement shows, Marx is by no means only concerned with the alienation of man from his product nor only with the alienation of work. He is concerned with man's alienation from life, from himself, and from his fellowman. This idea is expressed in the following: "Thus alienated labor turns the *species life of man,* and also nature as his mental species-property, into an *alien* being and into a *means* for his *individual existence.* It alienates from man his own body, external nature, his mental life, and his *human* life. A direct consequence of the alienation of man from the product of his labor from his life activity and from the species life is that man is *alienated* from other *men.* When man confronts himself he also confronts *other* men. What is true of man's relationship to his work, to the product of his work, and to himself, is also true of his relationship to other men, to their labor, and to the objects of their labor. In general,

---

[1] *Ibid.,* p. 101.
[2] *Ibid.,* p. 101.

the statement that man is alienated from his species life means that each man is alienated from others, and that each of the others is likewise alienated from human life." [1]

I must add to this presentation of Marx's concept of alienation as he expressed it in his *Economic and Philosophical Manuscripts* that the concept, although not the word, remains of central significance throughout his whole later main work, including *The Capital*. In the *German Ideology* Marx wrote: "As long as a cleavage exists between the particular and the common interest man's own deed becomes an alien power opposed to him, which enslaves him instead of being controlled by him." [2] And later: "This crystallization of social activity, this consolidation of what we ourselves produce into an objective power above us, growing out of our control, thwarting our expectations, bringing to naught our calculations, is one of the chief factors in historical development up to now." [3] Here follow some of the many statements in Capital dealing with alienation: "In handicraft and manufacture, the workman makes use of a tool; in the factory the machine makes use of him. There the movements of the instruments of labor proceed from him; here it is the movement of the machines that he must follow. In manufacture, the workmen are part of a living mechanism; in the factory, we have a lifeless mechanism, independent of the workman, who becomes its mere living appendage." [4, 5] Or (education of the future will) "com-

---

[1] *Ibid.*, p. 103.

[2] *German Ideology*, p. 220.

[3] *Ibid.*, pp. 22-23.

[4] *Capital I*, pp. 461-462.

[5] The whole problem of the continuity of the concept of alienation in Marx's thought has been treated excellently in R. Tucker's book *Philosophy and Myth* in Karl Marx. Cf. also the chapter on the continuity in Marx's thought in my *Marx's Concept of Man* (New York: Frederick Ungar Publishing Co., 1961).

bine productive labor with instruction and gymnastics, not only as one of the methods of adding to the efficiency of production, but as the only method of producing *fully developed human beings."* [1] Or: "Modern Industry, indeed, compels society, on the penalty of death, to replace the detail-worker of today, *crippled* by lifelong repetition of one and the same trivial operation, and thus reduced to the mere *fragment* of a man, by the *fully developed* individual . . . to whom the different social functions he performs are but so many *modes of giving free scope to his own natural and acquired powers."* [2] Alienation then, is, for Marx, *the* sickness of man. It is not a new sickness, since it starts necessarily with the beginning of division of labor, that is, of civilization transcending primitive society; it is most strongly developed in the working class yet it is a sickness from which everybody suffers. The sickness can be cured only when it has reached its peak; only the totally alienated man can overcome the alienation—he is forced to overcome his alienation since he cannot live as a totally alienated man and remain sane. Socialism is the answer; it is a society in which man becomes the conscious subject of history, experiences himself as the subject of his powers and thus emancipates himself from the bondage to things and circumstances. Marx gave expression to this idea of socialism and the realization of freedom in the following passage at the end of the third volume of Capital: "In fact, the realm of freedom does not commence until the point is passed where labor under the compulsion of necessity and of external utility is required. In the very nature of things it lies beyond the sphere of material production in the strict meaning of the term. Just as the savage must wrestle with nature, in order to satisfy his wants, in order to maintain

---

[1] *Capital I*, pp. 529-533 (My italics, E.F.).
[2] *Loc. cit.*, p. 534.

his life and reproduce it, so civilized man has to do it, and he must do it in all forms of society and under all possible modes of production. With his development the realm of natural necessity expands, because his wants increase; but at the same time the forces of production increase, by which these wants are satisfied. The freedom in this field cannot consist of anything else but of the fact that *socialized man, the associated producers, regulate their interchange with nature rationally, bring it under their common control, instead of being ruled by it as by some blind power;* that they accomplish their task with the least expenditure of energy and under conditions most adequate to their human nature and most worthy of it. *But it always remains a realm of necessity.* Beyond it begins that development of human power, which is its own end, the true realm of freedom, which, however, can flourish only upon that realm of necessity as its basis." [1]

We come closer to the problem of alienation as a moral and a psychological problem if we consider statements which Marx made in these two respects. For Marx alienation corrupts and perverts all human values. By making economic activities and the values inherent in them, like "gain, work, thrift and sobriety," [2] the supreme value of life, man fails to develop the truly moral values of humanity, "the riches of a good conscience, of virtue, etc., but how can I be virtuous if I am not alive and how can I have a good conscience if I am not aware of anything?" [3] In a state of alienation, each sphere of life, the economic and

---

[1] *Capital III*, p. 954.

[2] *Ibid.*, p. 146. Incidentally, these values are not only those of nineteenth-century capitalism, but they are the main values in contemporary Soviet Russia. Cf. a detailed discussion of this point in E. Fromm, *May Man Prevail?* (New York: Doubleday and Anchor Books, 1961)

[3] *Economic and Philosophical Manuscripts*, p. 146.

the moral, is independent from the other, "each is concentrated upon a specific area of alienated activity and is itself
alienated from the other." [1]

Marx foresaw with amazing clarity how the needs of man
in an alienated society would be perverted into true weaknesses. In capitalism, as Marx sees it, "Every man speculates upon creating a new need in another in order to force
him to a new sacrifice, to place him in a new dependence,
and to entice him into a new kind of pleasure and thereby
into economic ruin. Everyone tries to establish over others
an *alien* power in order to find there the satisfaction of his
own egoistic need. With the mass of objects, therefore,
there also increases the realm of alien entities to which man
is subjected. Every new product is a new *potentiality* of
mutual deceit and robbery. Man becomes increasingly poor
as a man; he has increasing need of *money* in order to take
possession of the hostile being. The power of *money* dimin-
ishes directly with the growth of the quantity of production, i.e., his need increases with the increasing *power* of
money. The need for money is therefore the real need
created by the modern economy, and the only need which
it creates. The *quantity* of money becomes increasingly its
only important quality. Just as it reduces every entity to
its abstraction, so it reduces itself in its own development
to a *quantitative* entity. Excess and immoderation become
its true standard. This is shown subjectively, partly in the
fact that the expansion of production and of needs becomes
an *ingenious* and always *calculating* subservience to inhuman, depraved, unnatural, and *imaginary* appetites. Private property does not know how to change crude need
into *human* need; its *idealism* is *fantasy, caprice* and *fancy*.
No eunuch flatters his tyrant more shamefully or seeks by
more infamous means to stimulate his jaded appetite, in

------
[1] *Ibid.*

order to gain some favor, than does the eunuch of industry, the entrepreneur, in order to acquire a few silver coins or to charm the gold from the purse of his dearly beloved neighbor. (Every product is a bait by means of which the individual tries to entice the essence of the other person, his money. Every real or potential need is a weakness which will draw the bird into the lime. As every imperfection of man is a bond with heaven, a point at which his heart is accessible to the priest, so every want is an opportunity for approaching one's neighbor with the air of friendship, and saying, 'Dear friend, I will give you what you need, but you know the *conditio sine qua non*. You know what ink you must use in signing yourself over to me. I shall swindle you while providing your enjoyment.' All this constitutes a universal exploitation of human communal life.) The entrepreneur accedes to the most depraved fancies of his neighbor, plays the role of pander between him and his needs, awakens unhealthy appetites in him, and watches for every weakness in order, later, to claim the remuneration for this labor of love." [1] The man who has thus become subject to his alienated needs is "a *mentally* and *physicaly dehumanized* being . . . the *self-conscious* and *self-acting commodity*." [2] This commodity-man knows only one way of relating himself to the world outside, by having it and by consuming (using) it. The more alienated he is, the more the sense of having and using constitutes his relationship to the world. "The less you *are*, the less you express your life, the more you *have*, the greater is your *alienated* life and the greater is the saving of your alienated being." [3]

Discussing Marx's concept of alienation, it might be of some interest to point to the close connection between the

---

[1] *Economic and Philosophical Manuscripts,* pp. 140–2.
[2] *Ibid.,* p. 111.
[3] *Ibid.,* p. 144.

phenomenon of alienation and the phenomenon of transference which is one of the most fundamental concepts in
Freud's system. Freud had observed that the psychoanalytic patient tended to fall in love with the analyst, to
be afraid of him, or to hate him, and all this quite without
regard to the reality of the analyst's personality. Freud believed that he had found the theoretical explanation to this
phenomenon by the assumption that the patient transferred the feelings of love, fear, hate, he had experienced
as a child toward father and mother, to the person of the
analyst. In the "transference," so Freud reasoned, the
child in the patient relates himself to the person of the
analyst as to his father or mother. Undoubtedly, Freud's
interpretation of the transference phenomenon has much
truth in it, and is supported by a good deal of evidence.
Yet it is not a complete interpretation. The grown-up
patient *is not* a child, and to talk about the child in
him, or "his" unconscious, is using a topological language which does not do justice to the complexity of the
facts. The neurotic, grown-up patient is an alienated human being; he does not feel strong, he is frightened and in-
hibited because he does not experience himself as the subject and originator of his own acts and experiences. He is
neurotic *because* he is alienated. In order to overcome his
sense of inner emptiness and impotence, he chooses an object onto whom he projects all his own human qualities:
his love, intelligence, courage, etc. By submitting to this
object, he feels in touch with his own qualities; he feels
strong, wise, courageous, and secure. To lose the object
means danger of losing himself. This mechanism, idolatric
worship of an object, based on the fact of the individual's
alienation, is the central dynamism of transference, that
which gives transference its strength and intensity. The less
alienated person may also transfer some of his infantile
experience to the analyst, but there would be little intensity

in it. The alienated patient, in search for and in need of an idol, finds the analyst and usually endows him with the qualities of his father and mother as the two powerful persons he knew as a child. Thus the *content* of transference is usually related to infantile patterns while its *intensity* is the result of the patient's alienation. Needless to add that the transference phenomenon is not restricted to the analytic situation. It is to be found in all forms of idolization of authority figures, in political, religious, and social life.

Tranference is not the only phenomenon of psychopathology which can be understood as an expression of alienation. Indeed, it is not accidental that *aliéné*, in French and *alienado* in Spanish, are older words for the psychotic, and the English "alienist" refers to a doctor who cares for the insane, the absolutely alienated person.[1]

Alienation as a sickness of the self can be considered to be the core of the psychopathology of modern man even in those forms which are less extreme than psychosis. Some clinical examples may serve to illustrate the process. The most frequent and obvious case of alienation is perhaps the false "great love." A man has fallen enthusiastically in love with a woman; after she had responded at first, she is beset by increasing doubts and breaks off the relationship. He is overcome by a depression which brings him close to suicide. Life, he feels, has no more meaning to him. Consciously he explains the situation as a logical result of what happened. He believes that for the first time he has experienced what real love is, that with this woman, and only with her, could he experience love and happiness. If she leaves him, there will never be anyone

---

[1] Cf. my discussion of this point in *The Sane Society*, p. 121ff. and in Tucker's *Philosophy and Myth in Karl Marx*, p. 144ff. Cf. also Karen Horney's remarks in *Neuroses and Human Growth* on the feeling of being driven but not driving and Tucker's references to Horney.

else who can arouse the same response in him. Losing her, so he feels, he has lost his one chance to love. Hence it is better to die. While all this sounds convincing to himself, his friends may ask some questions: Why is it that a man who thus far seemed less capable of loving than the average person is now so completely in love that he would rather die than live without his beloved? Why is it that although he is so completely in love he seems to be unwilling to make any concessions, to give up certain demands which conflict with those of the woman he loves? Why is it that while he speaks of his loss, he mainly speaks about himself and what has happened to him, and shows relatively little interest in the feelings of the woman he loves so much? If one speaks to the unhappy man himself, at greater length, one need not be surprised to hear him say at one point that he feels completely empty, so empty in fact as if he had left his heart with the girl he lost. If he can understand the meaning of his own statement he can understand that his predicament is one of alienation. He never was capable of loving actively, of leaving the magic circle of his own ego, and of reaching out to and becoming one with another human being. What he did was to transfer his longings for love to the girl and to feel that being with her he experiences his "loving" when he really experiences only the illusion of loving. The more he endows her not only with his longing for love but also for aliveness, happiness, and so on, the poorer he becomes, and the emptier he feels if he is separated from her. He was under the illusion of loving, when actually he had made the woman into an idol, the goddess of love, and believed that by being united with her he experienced love. He had been able to initiate a response in her but he had not been able to overcome his own inner muteness. Losing her is not, as he thinks, losing the person he loves, but losing himself as a potentially loving person.

Alienation of thought is not different from alienation of the heart. Often one believes he has thought through something, that his idea is the result of his own thinking activity; the fact is that he has transferred his brain to the idols of public opinion, the newspapers, the government or a political leader. He believes that they express his thoughts while in reality he accepts their thoughts as his own, because he has chosen them as his idols, his gods of wisdom and knowledge. Precisely for this reason he is dependent on his idols and incapable of giving up his worship. He is their slave because he has deposited his brain with them.

Another example of alienation is the alienation of hope, in which the future is transformed into an idol. This idolatry of history can be clearly seen in Robespierre's views. "O posterity, sweet and tender hope of humanity, thou art not a stranger to us; it is for thee that we brave all the blows of tyranny; it is thy happiness which is the price of our painful struggles: often discouraged by the obstacles that surround us, we feel the need of thy consolations; it is to thee that we confide the task of completing our labors, and the destiny of all the unborn generations of men! . . . Make haste, O posterity, to bring to pass the hour of equality, of justice, of happiness!" [1] Similarly, a distorted version of Marx's philosophy of history has often been used in the same sense by Communists. The logic of this argument is: whatever is in accord with the historical trend is necessary, hence good and vice versa. In this view, whether in the form of Robespierre's or the communist argument, it is not man who makes history but history that makes man. It is not man who hopes and has faith in the future but the future judges him and decides whether he had the right faith. Marx expressed very succinctly the opposite view of history to the alienated one

[1] Quoted by Carl L. Becker, *The Heavenly City of the Eighteenth-Century Philosophers,* pp. 142-3. Yale University Press, 1932.

I just quoted. "History," he wrote in *The Holy Family,* "does *nothing,* it possesses no colossal riches, it fights *no* battles! It is rather man, actual and living man, who does all this; 'history' does not use man as a means for *its* purposes as though it were a person apart; it is *nothing* but the activity of man pursuing his ends."

The phenomenon of alienation has other clinical aspects, which I can discuss only briefly. Not only are all forms of depression, dependence and idol worship (including the "fanatic") direct expressions of, or compensations for, alienation; the phenomenon of the failure to experience one's identity which is a central phenomenon at the root of psychopathological phenomena is also a result of alienation. Precisely because the alienated person has transformed his own functions of feeling and thought to an object outside he is not himself, he has no sense of "I," of identity. This lack of a sense of identity has many consequences. The most fundamental and general one is that it prevents integration of the total personality, hence it leaves the person disunited within himself, lacking either capacity "to will one thing" [1] or if he seems to will one thing his will lacks authenticity.

In the widest sense, every neurosis can be considered an outcome of alienation; this is so because neurosis is characterized by the fact that one passion (for instance, for money, power, women, etc.) becomes dominant and separated from the total personality, thus becoming the ruler of the person. This passion is his idol to which he submits even though he may rationalize the nature of his idol and give it many different and often well-sounding names. He is ruled by a partial desire, he transfers all he has left to this desire, he is weaker the stronger "it" becomes. He has

---

[1] Cf. S. Kierkegaard, *Purity of Heart is to Will One Thing,* Torch Books.

become alienated from himself precisely because "he" has become the slave of a part of himself.

Seeing alienation as a pathological phenomenon must, however, not obscure the fact that Hegel and Marx considered it a *necessary* phenomenon, one which is inherent in human evolution. This is true with regard to the alienation of reason as well as of love. Only when I can distinguish between the world outside and myself, that is, only if the world outside becomes an *object,* can I grasp it and make it my world, become one with it again. The infant, for whom the world is not yet conceived as "object," can also not grasp it with his reason and reunite himself with it. Man has to become alienated in order to overcome this split in the activity of his reason. The same holds true for love. As long as the infant has not separated himself from the world outside he is still part of it, and hence cannot love. In order to love, the "other" must become a stranger, and in the act of love, the stranger ceases to be a stranger and becomes me. Love presupposes alienation—and at the same time overcomes it. The same idea is to found in the prophetic concept of the Messianic Time and in Marx's concept of socialism. In Paradise man still is one with nature, but not yet aware of himself as separate from nature and his fellowman. By his act of disobedience man acquires self-awareness, the world becomes estranged from him. In the process of history, according to the prophetic concept, man develops his human powers so fully that eventually he will acquire a new harmony with men and nature. Socialism, in Marx's sense, can only come, once man has cut off all primary bonds, when he has become completely alienated and thus is able to reunite himself with men and nature without sacrificing his integrity and individuality.

The concept of alienation has its roots in a still earlier phase of the Western tradition, in the thought of the Old

Testament prophets, more specifically in their concept of *idolatry*. The prophets of monotheism did not denounce heathen religions as idolatrous primarily because they worshiped several gods instead of one. The essential difference between monotheism and polytheism is not one of the *numbers* of gods, but lies in the fact of alienation. Man spends his energy, his artistic capacities on building an idol, and then he worships this idol, which is nothing but the result of his own human effort. His life forces have flowed into a "thing," and this thing, having become an idol, is not experienced as a result of his own productive effort, but as something apart from himself, over and against himself, which he worships and to which he submits. As the prophet Hosea says (XIV, 8): "Assur shall not save us; we will not ride upon horses; neither will we say any more to the work of our hands, you are our gods; for in thee the fatherless finds love." Idolatrous man bows down to the work of his own hands. *The idol represents his own life-forces in an alienated form.*

The principle of monotheism, in contrast, is that man is infinite, that there is no partial quality in him which can be hypostatized into the whole. God, in the monotheistic concept, is unrecognizable and indefinable; God is not a "thing." Man being created in the likeness of God is created as the bearer of infinite qualities. In idolatry man bows down and submits to the projection of one partial quality in himself. He does not experience himself as the center from which living acts of love and reason radiate. He becomes a thing, his neighbor becomes a thing, just as his gods are things. "The idols of the heathen are silver and gold, the work of men's hands. They have mouths but they speak not; eyes have they, but they see not; they have ears but they hear not; neither is there any breath in their mouths. They that make them are like them; so is everyone that trusts in them." (Psalm 135)

Modern man, in industrial society, has changed the form and intensity of idolatry. He has become the object of blind economic forces which rule his life. He worships the work of his hands, he transforms himself into a thing. Not the working class alone is alienated (in fact, if anything, the skilled worker seems to be less alienated than those who manipulate men and symbols) but everybody is. This process of alienation which exists in the European-American industrialized countries, regardless of their political structure, has given rise to new protest movements. The renaissance of socialist humanism is one symptom of this protest. Precisely because alienation has reached a point where it borders on insanity in the whole industrialized world, undermining and destroying its religious, spiritual, and political traditions and threatening general destruction through nuclear war, many are better able to see that Marx had recognized the central issue of modern man's sickness; that he had not only seen, as Feuerbach and Kierkegaard had, this "sickness" but that he had shown that contemporary idolatry is rooted in the contemporary mode of production and can be changed only by the complete change of the economic-social constellation together with the spiritual liberation of man.

Surveying the discussion of Freud's and Marx's respective views on mental illness, it is obvious that Freud is primarily concerned with individual pathology, and Marx is concerned with the pathology common to a society and resulting from the particular system of that society. It is also clear that the content of psychopathology is quite different for Marx and for Freud. Freud sees pathology essentially in the failure to find a proper balance between the Id and Ego, between instinctual demands and the demands of reality; Marx sees the essential illness, as what the nineteenth century called *la maladie du siécle,* the estrangement of man from his own humanity and hence from his fellow man. Yet it is often overlooked that Freud by no means thought exclusively in terms of individual pathology. He speaks also of a "social neurosis." "If the evolution of civilization," he writes, "has such a far-reaching similarity with the development of an individual, and if the same methods are employed in both, would not the diagnosis be justified that many systems of civilization—or epochs of it —possibly even the whole of humanity—have become 'neurotic' under the pressure of civilizing trends? To analytic dissection of these neuroses, therapeutic recommendations might follow which could claim a great practical interest. I would not say that such an attempt to apply psychoanalysis to civilized society would be fanciful or doomed to fruitlessness. But it behooves us to be very careful, not to forget that after all we are dealing only with analogies, and that it is dangerous, not only with men but also with concepts, to drag them out of the region where they originated and have matured. The diagnosis of *collective neuroses,* moreover, will be confronted by a special difficulty. In the neurosis of an individual we can use as a starting point the contrast presented to us between the patient and his environment which we assume to be 'normal.' No such background as this would be available for any society similarly affected; it would have to be supplied in some other way. And with regard to any therapeutic application of our knowledge, what would be the use of the most acute analysis of social neuroses, since no one possesses the power to compel the community to adopt the therapy? In spite of all these difficulties, we may expect that one day someone will venture upon this *research into the pathology of civilized communities.*" [1]

---

[1] S. Freud, *Civilization and its Discontents,* translated from the German by J. Riviere (London: The Hogarth Press, Ltd., 1953), pp. 141–2. (Italics mine, E.F.)

But in spite of Freud's interest in the "social neuroses," [1] one fundamental difference between Freud's and Marx's thinking remains: Marx sees man as formed by his society, and hence sees the root of pathology in specific qualities of the social organization. Freud sees man as primarily formed by his experience in the family group; he appreciates little that the family is only the representative and agent of society, and he looks at various societies mainly in terms of the *quantity* of repression they demand, rather than the *quality* of their organization and of the impact of this social quality on the quality of the thinking and feeling of the members of a given society.

This discussion of the difference between Marx's and Freud's views on psychopathology, brief as it is, must mention one more aspect in which their thinking follows the same method. For Freud the state of primary narcissism of the infant, and the later oral and anal stages of libido development, are "normal" inasmuch as they are necessary stages in the process of evolution. The dependent, greedy infant is not a sick infant. Yet the dependent, greedy adult, who has been "fixated" on, or who has "regressed" to, the oral level of the child is a sick adult. The main needs and strivings are the same in the infant and in the adult; why then is the one healthy and the other sick? The answer lies quite obviously in the concept of evolution. What is normal at a certain stage is pathological at another stage. Or, to put it differently: what is *necessary* at one stage is also normal or rational. What is *unnecessary*, seen from the standpoint of evolution, is irrational and pathological. The adult who "repeats" an infantile stage at the same time does not and cannot repeat it, precisely because he is no longer a child.

---

[1] In my *The Sane Society* (New York: Rinehart & Company, Inc., 1955), I have attempted an analysis of the "social neurosis" of our time, of the "pathology of normalcy."

Marx following Hegel, employs the same method in viewing the evolution of man in society. Primitive man, medieval man, and the alienated man of industrial society are sick and yet not sick, because their stage of development is a necessary one. Just as the infant has to mature physiologically in order to become an adult, so the human race has to mature sociologically in the process of gaining mastery of nature and of society in order to become fully human. All irrationality of the past, while regrettable, is rational inasmuch as it was necessary. But when the human race stops at a stage of development which it should have passed, when it finds itself in contradiction with the possibilities which the historical situation offers, then its state of existence is irrational or, if Marx had used the term, pathological. Both Marx's and Freud's concepts of pathology can be understood fully only in terms of their evolutionary concept of individual and human history.

VII

THE CONCEPT OF MENTAL HEALTH

THUS far we have dealt with similarities and discrepancies in Marx's and Freud's views on individual and social *pathology*. We now have to examine what the respective similarities and differences are with regard to the concept of *mental health*.

Let us begin with Freud. For him, seen from one standpoint, only primitive man could be called "healthy." He satisfies all his instinctual demands without need for repression, frustration, or sublimation. (That Freud's picture of the primitive as having an unrestricted life filled with instinctual satisfaction is a romantic fiction has been made abundantly clear by contemporary anthropologists.) But when Freud turns from historical speculation to the clinical examination of contemporary man, this picture of primitive mental health hardly matters. Even if we would keep in mind that civilized man cannot be completely healthy (or happy, for that matter), Freud has nevertheless definite criteria for what constitutes mental health. These criteria are to be understood within the frame of reference of his evolutionary theory. This theory has two main aspects: the evolution of the libido, and the evolution of man's relations to others. In the theory of libido evolution Freud assumes that the libido, that is, the energy of the sexual drive, undergoes a development. It is at first centered around the oral activities of the child—sucking and biting—and later around the anal activities—elimination. Around the age of five or six, the libido has for the first time centered around the genital organs. But at this early age sexuality is not yet fully developed, and between the first "phallic phase" near the age of six and the beginning of puberty there is a "latency period," during which sexual development is at a standstill, as it were, and only at the beginning of puberty does the process of libido development come to its fruition.

This process of libido development, however, is by no means an uncomplicated one. Many events, especially oversatisfaction and overfrustration, can result in a child becoming "fixated" on the earlier level, and thus never arriving at a fully developed genital level, or regressing to an earlier one even after having arrived at the genital level. As a result, the adult may exhibit neurotic symptoms (like impotence), or neurotic character traits (as in the over-dependent, passive person). For Freud the "healthy" person is the one who has reached the "genital level" without regressing, and who lives an adult existence, that is, an existence in which he can work and have adequate sexual satisfaction or, to put it differently, in which he can produce things and reproduce the race.

The other aspect of the "healthy" person lies in the sphere of his object relations. The newborn baby has not yet any object relations. It is in a state of "primary narcissism" in which the only realities are his own bodily and mental experiences, and the world outside does not yet exist conceptually, and even less, emotionally. The child then develops his strong attachment to mother, an attachment which, at least in the case of the boy, develops into a sexual one, and is broken up by the fear of the father's castration threat. The child shifts from the fixation to

mother to the allegiance to father. At the same time, however, he also identifies with father by incorporating his
commands and prohibitions. Through this process he
achieves independence from father and from mother. The
healthy person, for Freud, then, is the one who has reached
the genital level, and who has become his own master, independent of father and mother, relying on his own reason
and on his own strength. But even though the main features of Freud's concept of mental health are clear, it cannot be denied that this concept remains somewhat vague
and certainly lacks the precision and penetration of his
concept of mental illness. It is actually the concept of a
well-functioning member of the middle class at the beginning of the twentieth century, who is sexually and economically potent.

Marx's picture of the healthy man is rooted in the humanistic concept of the independent, active, productive
man, as it was developed by Spinoza, Goethe, and Hegel.

The aspect in which Marx's and Freud's picture of the
healthy man coincide is that of *independence.* But Marx's
concept transcends that of Freud because Freud's independence is a limited one; the son makes himself independent of the father by incorporating his system of commandments and prohibitions; he carries fatherly authority within
himself and remains obedient to and dependent on the father and the social authorities in this indirect way. For
Marx independence and freedom are rooted in the act of
self-creation. "A being," Marx wrote, "does not regard
himself as independent unless he is his own master, and he
is only his own master when he owes his existence to himself. A man who lives by the favor of another considers
himself a dependent being. But I live completely by another person's favor when I owe to him not only the con-
tinuance of my life but also *its creation,* when he is its
source. My life has necessarily such a cause outside

itself if it is not my own creation." [1] Or, as Marx put it, man is independent only ". . . if he affirms his individuality as a total man in each of his relations to the world, seeing, hearing, smelling, tasting, feeling, thinking, willing, loving—in short, if he affirms and expresses all organs of his individuality"—if he is not only free *from* but also free *to*. For Marx, freedom and independence were not merely political and economic freedom in the sense of liberalism, but *the positive realization of individuality*. His concept of socialism was precisely that of a social order which serves the realization of the individual personality. Marx wrote: "[This crude communism] appears in a double form; the domination of material property looms so large that it aims to destroy everything which is incapable of being possessed by everyone as private property. It wishes to eliminate talent, etc., by *force*. Immediate physical possession seems to it the unique goal of life and existence. The role of *worker* is not abolished but is extended to all men. The relation of private property remains the relation of the community to the world of things. Finally, this tendency to oppose general private property to private property is expressed in an animal form; *marriage* (which is incontestably a form of *exclusive private property*) is contrasted with the community of women,[2] in which women become communal and common property. One may say that this idea of the *community of women* is the *open secret* of this entirely crude and unreflective communism. Just as women are to pass from marriage to universal prostitution, so the whole world of wealth (i.e., the objective being of man) is to pass to the relation of universal prostitution with the community. This communism,

---

[1] *Economic and Philosophical Manuscripts,* p. 138.

[2] Marx refers here to speculations among certain eccentric communist thinkers of his time who thought that if everything is common property women should be, too.

which negates the personality of man in every sphere, is the only logical expression of private property, which *is* this negation. Universal *envy* setting itself up as a power is only a camouflaged form of cupidity which reestablishes itself and satisfies itself in a different way. The thoughts of every individual private property are *at least* directed against any *wealthier* private property, in the form of envy and the desire to reduce everything to a common level; so that this envy and levelling in fact constitute the essence of competition. Crude communism is only the culmination of such envy and levelling-down on the basis of a *preconceived* minimum. How little the abolition of private property represents a genuine appropriation is shown by the abstract negation of the whole world of culture and civilization, and the regression to the *unnatural* simplicity of the poor and wantless individual who has not only not surpassed private property but has not yet even attained to it. The community is only a community of *work* and of *equality of wages* paid out by the communal capital, by the *community* as universal capitalist. The two sides of the relation are raised to a *supposed* universality; *labor* as a condition in which everyone is placed, and *capital* as the acknowledged universality and power of the community." [1]

Freud's independent man has emancipated himself from the dependence on mother; Marx's independent man has emancipated himself from the dependence on nature. However, there is one important difference between the two concepts of independence. Freud's independent man is basically a self-sufficient man. He needs others only as means to satisfy his instinctual desires. Since men and women need each other, this satisfaction is a mutual one. The relationship is not primarily but only secondarily a social one, like that of individual buyers and sellers on

---

[1] *Economic and Philosophical Manuscripts,* pp. 124–6.

the market who are united by their mutual interest in exchange. For Marx, man is primarily a social being. He is in need of his fellow man, not as a means to satisfy his desires, but because he is only he, he is only complete as a man, if he is related to his fellow men and to nature.[1]

The independent, free man in Marx's sense is, at the same time, the active, related, productive man. Spinoza, who had considerable influence on Marx, as he had on Hegel and Goethe, held activity vs. passivity to be central concepts for the understanding of man. He differentiated between active and passive emotions. The former (fortitude and generosity) originate in the individual, and they are accompanied by adequate ideas. The latter rule over man; he is the slave of passions and they are connected with inadequate, irrational ideas. This connection between knowledge and affect has been enriched by Goethe and Hegel in their emphasis on the nature of true knowledge. Knowledge is not obtained in the position of the split between subject and object, but in the position of relatedness. As Goethe put it: "Man knows himself only inasmuch as he knows the world. He knows the world only within himself, and he is aware of himself only within the world. Each new object, truly recognized, opens up a new organ within ourselves." [2] In his *Faust,* Goethe gave the most outstanding expression to this concept of the "ever striving" man. Neither knowledge nor power nor sex can give an ultimately satisfactory answer to the question which man is asked by the fact of his very existence. Only the free and productive man, united to his fellow man, can give the right answer to man's existence, Marx's concept of man was a dynamic one. Human passion is, he said, "the

---

[1] It was Alfred Adler who emphasized the fundamental social nature of man, even though he has not given the concept the depth it has in Marx and in German enlightenment thinking.

[2] *Conversations with Eckermann,* January 29, 1826.

essential power of man striving energetically for its object."
Man's own powers develop only in the process of relatedness to the world. "The eye has become a *human* eye when
its *object* has become a *human,* social object, created by
man and destined for him. The senses have therefore become directly theoreticians in practice They relate themselves to the thing for the sake of the thing, but the thing
itself is an *objective human* relation to itself and to man
and vice versa. Need and enjoyment have thus lost their
egoistic character, and nature has lost its mere *utility* by the
fact that its utilization has become *human* utilization. (In
practice I can only relate myself in a human way to a thing
when the thing is related in a human way to man.)" [1]

Just as our senses develop and become human senses
in the process of their productive relatedness to nature, our
relatedness to man, says Marx, becomes human relatedness in the act of loving. "Let us assume *man* to be *man,*
and his relation to the world to be a human one. Then love
can only be exchanged for love, trust for trust, etc. If you
wish to enjoy art you must be an artistically cultivated person; if you wish to influence other people you must be a
person who really has a stimulating and encouraging effect
upon others. Every one of your relations to man and to
nature must be a *specific expression,* corresponding to the
object of your will, of your *real individual* life. If you love
without evoking love in return, i.e., if you are not able, by
the *manifestation* of yourself as a loving person, to make
yourself a *beloved person,* then your love is impotent and
a misfortune." [2]

The fully developed, and thus the healthy, man, is the
productive man, the man who is genuinely interested in the
world, responding to it; he is the rich man. In contrast to

---

[1] *Economic and Philosophical Manuscripts,* p. 132.
[2] *Ibid.,* p. 168.

this fully developed man, Marx paints the picture of man under the system of capitalism. "The production of too many useful things results in too many *useless* people." [1] In the present system man *has* much, but he *is* little. The fully developed man is the wealthy man who *is* much. "Communism," for Marx, "is the *positive* abolition of *private property,* [2] of *human self-alienation,* and thus the real *appropriation* of human nature through and for man. It is, therefore, the return of man himself as a *social,* i.e., really human being, a complete and conscious return which assimilates all the wealth of previous development. Communism as a fully developed naturalism is humanism and, as a fully developed humanism, is naturalism. It is the *definitive* resolution of the antagonism between man and nature, and between man and man. It is the true solution of the conflict between existence and essence, between objectification and self-affirmation, between freedom and necessity, between individual and species. It is the solution of the riddle of history and knows itself to be this solution." [3]

---

[1] *Ibid.,* p. 145.

[2] By "private property" as used here and in other statements, Marx never refers to the personal property of things for use (such as a house, table, etc.). He refers to the property of the "propertied classes," that is, of the capitalist who, because he owns the means of production, can hire the property-less individual to work for him, under conditions the latter is forced to accept. "Private property" in Marx's usage, then, always refers to private *property within capitalist class society* and thus is a *social and historical category;* the term does not refer to things for use, to "personal property."

[3] *Economic and Philosophical Manuscripts,* p. 127.

VIII

INDIVIDUAL AND SOCIAL CHARACTER

MARX postulated the interdependence between the economic basis of society and the political and legal institutions, its philosophy, art, religion, etc. The former, according to Marxist theory, determined the latter, the "ideological superstructure." But Marx and Engels did not show, as Engels admitted quite explicitly, *how* the economic basis is translated into the ideological superstructure. I believe that by using the tools of psychoanalysis, this gap in Marxian theory can be filled, and that it is possible to show the mechanisms through which the economic basic structure and the superstructure are connected. One of these connections lies in what I have called the *social character,* the other in the nature of the *social unconscious* to be dealt with in the next chapter.

In order to explain the concept of "social character" we must first survey one of the most significant of Freud's discoveries: his *dynamic* concept of character. Until Freud, character traits were considered by the behavioristically oriented psychologists to be synonymous with behavior traits. From this standpoint, character is defined as "the pattern of behavior characteristic for a given individual," [1] while other authors like William McDougall, R. G. Gordon,

---

[1] Leland E. Hinsie and Jacob Shatzky, *Psychiatric Dictionary* (New York: Oxford University Press, 1940).

and Kretschmer have emphasized the conative and dynamic element of character traits.

Freud developed not only the first but also a most consistent and penetrating theory of character as a system of strivings which underlie, but are not identical with, behavior. In order to appreciate Freud's dynamic concept of character, a comparison between behavior traits and character traits will be helpful. Behavior traits are described in terms of actions which are observable by a third person. Thus, for instance, the behavior trait "being courageous" would be defined as behavior which is directed toward reaching a certain goal without being deterred by risks to one's comfort, freedom, or life. Or parsimony as a behavior trait would be defined as behavior which aims at saving money or other material things. However, if we inquire into the motivation and particularly into the unconscious motivation of such behavior traits, we find that the *behavior* trait covers numerous and entirely different *character* traits. Courageous behavior may be motivated by ambition so that a person will risk his life in certain situations in order to satisfy his craving for being admired; it may be motivated by suicidal impulses which drive a person to seek danger because, consciously or unconsciously, he does not value his life and wants to destroy himself; it may be motivated by sheer lack of imagination so that a person acts courageously because he is not aware of the danger awaiting him; finally, it may be determined by genuine devotion to the idea or aim for which a person acts, a motivation which is conventionally assumed to be the basis of courage. Superficially the behavior in all these instances is the same in spite of the different motivations. I say "superficially" because if one can observe such behavior minutely, one finds that the difference in motivation results also in subtle yet significant differences in behavior. An officer in battle, for instance, will behave quite differently in different situations if his courage is motivated by devotion to an idea rather than by ambition. In the first case he would not attack in certain situations if the risks are in no proportion to the tactical ends to be gained. If, on the other hand, he is driven by vanity, this passion may make him blind to the dangers threatening him and his soldiers. His behavior trait of "courage" in the latter case is obviously a very ambiguous asset. Another illustration is parsimony. A person may be economical because his economic circumstances make it necessary; or he may be parsimonious because he has a stingy character which makes saving an aim for its own sake, regardless of the realistic necessity. Here, too, the motivation would make some difference with regard to behavior itself. In the first case, the person would be very well able to discern a situation where it is wise to save from one in which it is wiser to spend money. In the latter case he will save regardless of the objective need for it. Another factor which is determined by the difference in motivation refers to the prediction of behavior. In the case of a "courageous" soldier motivated by ambition we may predict that he will behave courageously only if his courage can be rewarded. In the case of the soldier who is courageous because of devotion to his cause, we can predict that the question of whether or not his courage will find recognition will have little influence on his behavior.

Freud had recognized something that the great novelists and dramatists had always known: that, as Balzac put it, the study of character deals with "the forces by which man is motivated," that the way a person acts, feels, and thinks is to a large extent determined by the specificity of his character and is not merely the result of rational responses to realistic situations. Freud recognized the dynamic quality of character traits, and that the character structure of a person represents a particular form in which energy is canalized in the process of living.

Freud tried to account for this dynamic nature of character traits by combining his characterology with his libido theory. By a number of complicated and brilliant assumptions, he explained different character traits as "sublimations" of, or "reaction formations" against, the various forms of the sexual drive. He interpreted the *dynamic nature* of character traits as an expression of their *libidinous source.*

The character orientation, in Freud's sense, is the source of men's actions and of many of his ideas. Character is the equivalent of the animal's instinctive determination which man has lost. Man acts and thinks according to his character, and it is precisely for this reason that "character is man's fate," as Heraclitus put it. Man is motivated to act and to think in certain ways by his character, and at the same time he finds satisfaction in the very fact that he does so.

The character structure determines action, as well as thoughts and ideas. Let us take a few examples: for the anal-hoarding character, the ideal of saving is most attractive and, in fact, he tends to regard saving as one of the major virtues. He will like a way of life in which saving is encouraged and waste prohibited. He will tend to interpret situations in terms of his dominant striving. A decision, for instance, of whether to buy a book, go to a movie, or what to eat, will mainly be made in terms of "what is economical," quite regardless of whether his own economic circumstances warrant such a principle of choice or not. He also will interpret concepts in the same way. Equality means to him that everybody has exactly the same share of material goods and not, as it would mean to others of a different character, that men are equal inasmuch as no man must be made the means for the purposes of another.

A person with an oral-receptive character orientation

feels "the source of all good" to be outside, and he believes that the only way to get what he wants—be it something material, be it affection, love, knowledge, pleasure—is to receive it from that outside source. In this orientation the problem of love is almost exclusively that of "being loved" and not that of loving. Such people tend to be indiscriminate in the choice of their love objects, because being loved by anybody is such an overwhelming experience for them, that they "fall for" anybody who gives them love or what looks like love. They are exceedingly sensitive to any withdrawal or rebuff they experience on the part of the loved person. Their orientation is the same in the sphere of thinking. If intelligent, they make the best listeners, since their orientation is one of receiving, not of producing, ideas; left to themselves, they feel paralyzed. It is characteristic of these people that their first thought is to find somebody else to give them needed information, rather than to make even the smallest effort of their own. If religious, these persons have a concept of God in which they expect everything from God and nothing from their own activity. If not religious, their relationship to persons or institutions is very much the same; they are always in search of a "magic helper." They show a particular kind of loyalty, at the bottom of which is the gratitude for the hand that feeds them and the fear of ever losing it. Since they need many hands to feel secure, they have to be loyal to numerous people. It is difficult for them to say no, and they are easily caught between conflicting loyalties and promises. Since they cannot say no, they love to say yes to everything and everybody, and the resulting paralysis of their critical abilities makes them increasingly dependent on others. They are dependent not only on authorities for knowledge and help but also on people in general for any kind of support. They feel lost when alone because they feel that they cannot do anything without help. This helplessness is especially important with regard to those acts which, by their very nature, can only be done alone—making decisions and taking responsibility. In personal relationships, for instance, they ask advice from the very person with regard to whom they have to make a decision.

The exploitative orientation, like the receptive, has as its basic premise the feeling that the source of all good is outside, that whatever one wants to get must be sought there, and that one cannot produce anything oneself. The difference between the two, however, is that the exploitative type does not expect to receive things from others as a gift, but to take them by force or cunning. This orientation extends to all spheres of activity. In the realm of love and affection, these people tend to grab and steal; they tend to fall in love with a person attached to someone else. We find the same attitude with regard to thinking and intellectual pursuits. Such people will tend not to produce ideas but to steal them. This may be done directly in the form of plagiarism or, more subtly, by repeating in different phraseology the ideas voiced by others and insisting they are new and their own. It is a striking fact that frequently people with great intelligence proceed in this way, although if they relied on their own gifts they might well be able to have ideas of their own. The lack of original ideas or independent production in otherwise gifted people often has its explanation in this character orientation, rather than in any innate lack of originality. The same statement holds true with regard to their orientation in material things. Things which they can take from others always seem better to them than anything they can produce themselves. They use and exploit anybody and anything from whom or from which they can squeeze something. Their motto is "Stolen fruits are sweetest." Because they want to use and exploit people, they "love" those

who, explicitly or implicitly, are promising objects of
exploitation, and get "fed up" with persons whom they
have squeezed dry. An extreme example is the klepto-
maniac who enjoys things only if he can steal them, although he has the money to buy them.

It was necessary to describe in detail Freud's dynamic
concept of character in order to prepare the ground for
the discussion of the social character.

Individuals within a given society differ, of course, in
their personal characters; in fact it is no exaggeration to
say that if we are concerned with minute differences,
there are no two people whose character structure is identical. Yet if we disregard minute differences, we can form
certain types of character structures which are roughly
representative for various groups of individuals. Such
types are the receptive, the exploitative, the hoarding,
the marketing, the productive, character orientations.[1] The
problem of character structure gains in importance far
beyond the individual, if it can be shown that nations or
societies or classes within a given society have a character
structure which is characteristic for them, even though
individuals differ in many specific ways, and even though
there will be always a number of individuals whose character structure does not fit at all into the broader pattern
of the structure common to the group as a whole. I have
named this character which is typical for a society the
"social character."

Like the individual character, the "social character"
represents the specific way in which energy is channelized;
it follows that if the energy of most people in a given society is channelized in the same direction, their motivations
are the same, and furthermore, that they are receptive to
the same ideas and ideals. I shall try to show in the follow-

[1] Cf. the detailed discussion of these orientations in E. Fromm,
Man for Himself (New York: Rinehart & Company, Inc., 1947).

ing pages that "social character" is an essential element in the functioning of a society, and at the same time the transmission belt between the economic structure of society and the prevailing ideas.

What is the social character? I refer in this concept to *the nucleus of the character structure which is shared by most members of the same culture*, in contradistinction to the *individual character in which people belonging to the same culture differ from each other*. The concept of social character is not a statistical concept in the sense that it is simply the sum total of character traits to be found in the majority of people in a given culture. It can be understood only in reference to the *function* of the social character which we shall now proceed to discuss.[1]

Each society is structuralized and operates in certain ways which are necessitated by a number of objective conditions. These conditions include methods of production which in turn depend on raw materials, industrial techniques, climate, size of population, and political and geographical factors, cultural traditions and influences to which the society is exposed. There is no "society" in general, but only specific social structures which operate in different and ascertainable ways. Although these social structures do change in the course of historical development, they are relatively fixed at any given historical period; any society can exist only by operating within the framework of its particular structure. The

---

[1] In the following pages I have drawn on my paper, "Psychoanalytic Characterology and its Application to the Understanding of Culture," in *Culture and Personality*, ed. by G. S. Sargent and M. Smith, Viking Fund, 1949, pp. 1-12. The concept of the social character was developed originally in my "The Evolution of the Dogma of Christ," Intern. Psychoanalytischer Verlag, Vienna, 1931, and in "Die psychoanalytische Charakterologie und ihre Bedeutung für die Soziologie" in *Zeitschrift für Sozialforschung*, I. Hirschfeld, Leipzig, 1932.

members of the society and/or the various classes or status groups within it have to behave in such a way as to be able to function in the sense required by the social system. It is the function of the social character to shape the energies of the members of society in such a way that their behavior is not a matter of conscious decision as to whether or not to follow the social pattern, but one of *wanting to act as they have to act* and at the same time finding gratification in acting according to the requirements of the culture. In other words, it is the social character's function *to mold and channel human energy within a given society for the purpose of the continued functioning of this society.*

Modern, industrial society, for instance, could not have attained its ends had it not harnessed the energy of free men for work in an unprecedented degree. Man had to be molded into a person who was eager to spend most of his energy for the purpose of work, who had the qualities of discipline, orderliness and punctuality, to a degree unknown in most other cultures. It would not have sufficed if each individual had to make up his mind consciously every day that he wanted to work, to be on time, etc., since any such conscious deliberation would lead to many more exceptions than the smooth functioning of society can afford. Nor would threat and force have sufficed as a motive since the highly differentiated tasks in modern industrial society can, in the long run, only be the work of free men and not of forced labor. The social *necessity* for work, for punctuality, and orderliness had to be transformed into an inner *drive*. This means that society had to produce a social character in which these strivings were inherent.

While the need for punctuality and orderliness are traits necessary for the functioning of any industrial system, there are other needs which differ, say, in nineteenth-century capitalism, as against contemporary capitalism. Nineteenth-century capitalism was still mainly occupied with the accumulation of capital, and hence with the necessity of saving; it had to fortify discipline and stability by an authoritarian principle in the family, religion, industry, state and church. The social character of the nineteenth-century middle class was precisely one which in many ways can be called the "hoarding orientation." Abstention from consumption, saving, and respect for authority were not only virtues but they were also satisfactions for the average member of the middle classes; his character structure made him like to do what, for the purposes of his economic system, he had to do. The contemporary social character is quite different; today's economy is based not on restriction of consumption, but on its fullest development. Our economy would face a severe crisis if people—the working and the middle classes—were not to spend most of their income on consumption, rather than to save it. Consuming has become not only the passionate aim of life for most people, but it has also become a virtue. The modern consumer—the man who buys on installments—would have appeared an irresponsible and immoral waster to his grandfather, just as the latter would appear an ugly miser to his grandson. The nineteenth-century social character is to be found today only in the more backward social strata of Europe and North America; this social character can be defined as one for whom the principal aim was *having;* the twentieth-century social character is one for whom the aim is *using.*

A similar difference exists with regard to the forms of authority. In this century, at least in the developed capitalistic countries of the West, there is enough material satisfaction for all, and hence less need for authoritarian control. At the same time control has shifted into the hands of bureaucratic élites which govern less by enforcing obedience than by eliciting consent, a consent, however, which is to a large degree manipulated by the modern devices of psychology and a "science" called "human relations."

As long as the objective conditions of the society and the culture remain stable, the social character has a predominantly stabilizing function. If the external conditions change in such a way that they no longer fit the traditional social character, a *lag* arises which often changes the function of character into an element of disintegration instead of stabilization, into dynamite instead of a social mortar, as it were.

In speaking of the socio-economic structure of society as molding one's character, we speak only of one pole in the interconnection between social organization and man. The other pole to be considered is man's nature, molding in turn the social conditions in which he lives. The social process can be understood only if we start out with the knowledge of the reality of man, his psychic properties as well as his physiological ones, and if we examine the interaction between the nature of man and the nature of the external conditions under which he lives, and which he has to master if he is to survive.

While it is true that man can adapt himself to almost any conditions, he is not a blank sheet of paper on which the culture writes its text. Needs like the striving for happiness, belonging, love, and freedom are inherent in his nature. They are also dynamic factors in the historical process. If a social order neglects or frustrates the basic human needs beyond a certain threshold, the members of such a society will try to change the social order so as to make it more suitable to their human needs. If this change is not possible, the outcome will probably be that such a society will collapse, because of its lack of vitality, and its destructiveness. Social changes which lead to a

greater satisfaction of human needs are easier to make
when certain material conditions are given which facilitate
such changes. It follows from these considerations that the
relation between social change and economic change is
not only the one which Marx emphasized, namely, the
interests of new classes in changed social and political
conditions, but that social changes are at the same time
determined by the fundamental human needs which make
use, as it were, of favorable circumstances for their realization. The middle class which won the French revolution wanted freedom for their economic pursuits from the
fetters of the old order. But they also were driven by a
genuine wish for human freedom inherent in them as
human beings. While most were satisfied with a narrow
concept of freedom after the revolution had won, the
very best spirits of the bourgeoisie became aware of the
limitations of bourgeois freedom and, in their search for
a more satisfactory answer to man's needs, arrived at a
concept which considered freedom to be the condition for
the unfolding of the total man.

Provided this concept of the genesis and function of
the social character is correct, we are confronted with a
puzzling problem. Is not the assumption that the character structure is molded by the role which the individual
has to play in his culture contradicted by the assumption
that a person's character is molded in his childhood? Can
both views pretend to be true in view of the fact that the
child in his early years of life has comparatively little contact with society as such? This question is not as difficult
to answer as it may seem at first glance. We must differ-
entiate between the factors which are responsible for the
particular *contents* of the social character and the *methods*
by which the social character is produced. The structure
of society and the function of the individual in the social
structure may be considered to determine the content of

the social character. The family, on the other hand, may be considered to be the *psychic agency of society,* the institution which has the function of transmitting the requirements of society to the growing child. The family fulfills this function in two ways: (1) by the influence the character of the parents has on the character formation of the growing child; since the *character* of most parents is an expression of the social character, they transmit in this way the essential features of the socially desirable character structure to the child. (2) In addition to the character of the parents, the *methods of childhood training* which are customary in a culture also have the function of molding the character of the child in a socially desirable direction. There are various methods and techniques of child training which can fulfill the same end and, on the other hand, there can be methods which *seem* identical but which nevertheless are different because of the character structure of those who practice these methods. By focusing on methods of child training, we can never explain the social character. Methods of child training are significant only as a mechanism of *transmission,* and they can be understood correctly only if we understand first what kinds of personalities are desirable and necessary in any given culture.

Thus far we have looked at the social character as the structure through which human energy is molded in such specific ways, that it is usable for the purposes of any given society. We have now to show that it is also the basis from which certain ideas and ideals draw their strength and attractiveness. This relation between character and ideas, which has been mentioned before, is easy to recognize in the case of the individual character structure. A person with a hoarding (anal, according to Freud) character orientation, will be attracted to the ideal of saving, he will be repelled by ideas of what he would call "reckless spending." On the other hand, the person with a productive character will find a philosophy centered around saving "dirty," and will embrace ideas which emphasize creative efforts and the use of material goods as far as they enrich life. As far as the social character is concerned, the relationship between character and ideas is the same. Some examples ought to show this relation clearly. With the end of the feudal age, private property became the central factor in the economic and social system. There had been, of course, private property before. But in feudalism private property consisted largely in land, and it was connected to the social station of the landowner in the hierarchic system. It was not salable on the market since it was part of the social role of the owner. Modern capitalism destroyed the feudal system. Private property is not only property in land, it is also property in the means of production. All property is alienable; it can be bought and sold on the market, and its value is expressed in an abstract form—that of money. Land, machines, gold, diamonds—they all have in common the abstract money form in which their value can be expressed. Anybody can acquire private property, regardless of his position in the social system. It may be through industriousness, creativeness, luck, ruthlessness, or inheritance—the ownership of private property is not affected by the means of its acquisition. The security, power, sense of strength of a person does not, as in the feudal system, depend any longer on a person's status, which was relatively unalterable, but on the possession of private property. If the man of the modern era loses his private property he is nobody—socially speaking; the feudal lord could not lose it as long as the feudal system remained intact. As a result, the respective ideals are different. For the feudal lord, and even for the artisan belonging to a guild, the main concern was the stability of the traditional order, the harmonious relation to his superiors, the concept of a

God who was the final guarantor of the stability of the feudal system. If any of these ideas were attacked, a member of feudal society would even risk his life in order to defend what he considered to be his deepest convictions.

For modern man the ideals are quite different. His fate, security, and power rest on private property; hence for bourgeois society, private property is sacred, and the ideal of the invulnerability of private property is a cornerstone in its ideological edifice. Although the majority of people in any of the capitalist societies do not own private property in the sense used here (property in the means of production), but only "personal" property such as a car, television set, etc.—that is, consumer goods—the great bourgeois revolution against the feudal order has nevertheless formulated the principle of the invulnerability of private property so that even those who do not belong to the economic élite have the same feeling, in this respect, as those who belong. Just as the member of the feudal society considered an attack against the feudal system immoral, and even inhuman, so the average person in a capitalist society considers an attack against private property a sign of barbarism and inhumanity. He will often not say so directly but rationalize his hate against the violators of private property in terms of their godlessness, injustice, and so on; yet, in reality, and often unconsciously, they appear to him as inhuman because they have violated the sanctity of private property. The point is not that they have hurt him economically, or that they even threaten his economic interests realistically; the point is that they threaten a vital ideal. It seems, for instance, that the repugnance and hate which so many people in capitalistic countries have against the communist countries is, to a large extent, based on the very repugnance they feel against the outright violators of private property.

There are so many other examples of ideas which are

rooted in the socio-economic structure of a society that it is hard to select the most representative ones. Thus, liberty became the paramount idea for a middle class fighting against the restrictions that the feudal class imposed upon them. "Individual initiative" became an ideal in the highly competitive capitalism of the nineteenth century. Teamwork and "human relations" became the ideals of the capitalism of the twentieth century. "Fairness" became the most popular norm in capitalist society since fairness is the basic law of the free market in which commodities and labor are exchanged without force or fraud. At the same time, the idea of fairness became identified with an older norm, "love thy neighbor," via the popularized version of this norm in the form of the Golden Rule, "Do unto others as you would have them do unto you."

I want to emphasize again that the theory that ideas are determined by the forms of economic and social life does not imply that they have no validity of their own, or that they are mere "reflexes" of economic needs. The ideal of freedom, for instance, is deeply rooted in the nature of man, and it is precisely for this reason that it was an ideal for the Hebrews in Egypt, the slaves in Rome, the German peasants in the sixteenth century, the German workers who fought the dictators of East Germany. On the other hand, the idea of authority and order is also deeply implanted in human existence. It is precisely because any given social order can appeal to ideas which transcend the necessities of this order that they can become so potent and so appealing to the human heart. Yet why a certain idea gains ascendance and popularity is to be understood in historical terms, that is, in terms of the social character produced in a given culture.

One more qualification must be made. It is not only the "economic basis" which creates a certain social character which, in turn, creates certain ideas. The ideas, once created, also influence the social character and, indirectly, the social economic structure. What I emphasize here is *that the social character is the intermediary between the socio-economic structure and the ideas and ideals prevalent in a society.* It is the intermediary in both directions, from the economic basis to the ideas and from the ideas to the economic basis.[1]

The following scheme expresses this concept:

ECONOMIC BASIS

SOCIAL CHARACTER

IDEAS AND IDEALS

---

[1] In *Escape from Freedom* (New York: Rinehart & Company, Inc., 1941), I tried to show this mechanism in detail with regard to the connection of Protestantism and the beginning of capitalism. In *The Sane Society* (New York: Rinehart & Company, Inc., 1955), I dealt with the same problem in reference to the nineteenth and twentieth centuries.

IX

THE SOCIAL UNCONSCIOUS

THE social character which makes people act and think as they have to act and think from the standpoint of the proper functioning of their society is only one link between the social structure and ideas. The other link lies in the fact that each society determines which thoughts and feelings shall be permitted to arrive at the level of awareness and which have to remain unconscious. Just as there is a social character, there is also a *"social unconscious."*

By "social unconscious" I refer to those areas of repression which are common to most members of a society; these commonly repressed elements are those contents which a given society cannot permit its members to be aware of if the society with its specific contradictions is to operate successfully. The *"individual unconscious"* with which Freud deals refers to those contents which an individual represses for reasons of individual circumstances peculiar to his personal life situation. Freud deals to some extent with the "social unconscious" when he talks about the repression of incestuous strivings as being characteristic of all civilization; but in his clinical work, he mainly deals with the individual unconscious, and little attention is paid by most analysts to the "social unconscious."

Before I can begin to discuss the "social unconscious," it is necessary to present briefly the concept of the unconscious as Freud developed it, and the corresponding concept in Marx's system.

There is, indeed, no more fundamental discovery of Freud's than that of the unconscious. Psychoanalysis can be defined as a system which is based on the assumption that we repress the awareness of the most significant experiences; that the conflict between the unconscious reality within ourselves and the denial of that reality in our consciousness often leads to neurosis, and that by making the unconscious conscious, the neurotic symptom or character trait can be cured. While Freud believed that this uncovering of the unconscious was the most important tool for the therapy of neurosis, his vision went far beyond this therapeutic interest. He saw how unreal most of what we think about ourselves is, how we deceive ourselves continuously about ourselves and about others; he was prompted by the passionate interest to touch the reality which is behind our conscious thought. Freud recognized that *most of what is real within ourselves is not conscious, and that most of what is conscious is not real.* This devotion to the search for inner reality opened up a new dimension of truth. The person who does not know the phenomenon of the unconscious is convinced he says the truth if he says what he knows. Freud showed that we all deceive ourselves to a larger or smaller degree about the truth. Even if we are sincere with regard to what we are aware of, we are probably still lying because our consciousness is "false," it does not represent the underlying real experience within ourselves.

Freud started out with observation on an individual scale. Here are some random examples: a man may have a secret pleasure in looking at pornographic pictures. He does not admit any such interest to himself but is convinced, consciously, that he considers such pictures to be harmful and that it is his duty to see to it that they are not exhibited anywhere. In this way he is constantly concerned with pornography, looks at such pictures as part of his campaign against them, and thus satisfies his desire. But he has a very good conscience. His real desires are unconscious, and what is conscious is a rationalization which hides completely what he does not want to know. Thus he is enabled to satisfy his desire without sensing the conflict with his moral judgment. Another example would be that of a father with sadistic impulses, who tends to punish and mistreat his children. But he is convinced that he beats them because that is the only way to teach them virtue and to protect them from doing evil. He is not aware of any sadistic satisfaction—he is only aware of the rationalization, his idea of duty and of the right method of bringing up children. Here is still another example: a political leader may conduct a policy which leads to war. He may be motivated by a wish for his own glory and fame, yet he is convinced that his actions are determined exclusively by his patriotism and his sense of responsibility to his country. In all these instances the underlying and unconscious desire is so well rationalized by a moral consideration that the desire is not only covered up, but also aided and abetted by the very rationalization the person has invented. In the normal course of his life, such a person will never discover the contradiction between the reality of his desires and the fiction of his rationalizations, and hence he will go on acting according to his desire. If anyone would tell him the truth, that is to say, mention to him that behind his sanctimonious rationalizations are the very desires which he bitterly disapproves of, he would sincerely feel indignant or misunderstood and falsely accused. This passionate refusal to admit the existence of what is repressed, Freud called "resistance." Its strength is roughly in proportion to the strength of the repressive tendencies.

Naturally, while every kind of experience can be repressed, it follows from Freud's theoretical frame of reference that in his view the strivings which are most severely repressed are the sexual ones which are incompatible with the norms of civilized man, and first of all the incestuous strivings. But according to Freud, hostile and aggressive strivings also are repressed inasmuch as they are in conflict with the existing mores and the super-ego. Whatever the specific contents of the repressed strivings are, in Freud's view they represent always the "dark" side of man, the antisocial, primitive equipment of man which has not been sublimated, and which is in contrast to what man believes to be civilized and decent. It must be stressed again that in Freud's concept of the unconscious, repression means that the *awareness* of the impulse has been repressed, not the impulse itself; in the case of sadistic impulses, for instance, this means that I am not aware of my wish to inflict pain on others. However, this does not necessarily mean that I do not inflict pain upon others, provided that I can rationalize it as duty, or that I inflict pain on others without being aware that they suffer from my actions. There is also the possibility that the impulse is not acted upon precisely because I could not prevent myself from being aware of it, nor find a fitting rationalization. In this case the impulse will still exist, but the repression of its awareness will lead to its suppression as far as acting upon it is concerned. In any case, repression means a distortion in man's consciousness, it does not mean the removal of forbidden impulses from existence. It means that the unconscious forces have gone underground and determine man's actions behind his back.

What, according to Freud, causes repression? We have

said already that those impulses are prevented from becoming conscious which are incompatible with existing
social or family mores. This statement refers to the *contents* of repression; but what is the *psychological mechanism* through which the act of repression is possible?
According to Freud, this mechanism is *fear*. The most
representative example in Freud's theory is that of the
repression of the boy's incestuous strivings toward his
mother. Freud assumes that the little boy becomes afraid
of his rival—father—and, specifically, that father will
castrate him. This fear makes him repress the awareness
of the desire and helps him channel his desires in other
directions, although the scar of the first fright never entirely disappears. While "castration fear" is the most ele-
mentary fear leading to repression, other fears such as
that of not being loved or of being killed or abandoned
can, according to Freud, have the same power as the
original castration fear, namely, to force man to repress
his deepest desires.

While in individual psychoanalysis, Freud would look
for the individual factors of repression, it would nevertheless be erroneous to assume that his concept of repression is to be understood only in individual terms. On
the contrary, Freud's concept of repression also has a social dimension. The more society develops into higher
forms of civilization, the more instinctive desires become
incompatible with the existing social norms, and thus the
more repression must take place. Increasing civilization, to
Freud, means increasing repression. But Freud never went
beyond this quantitative and mechanistic concept of society and he did not examine the specific structure of a
society and its influence on repression.

If the forces which cause repression are so powerful,
how did Freud ever hope to make the unconscious conscious, to "derepress" the repressed? It is well known that

the psychoanalytic therapy he devised serves precisely this end. By analyzing dreams, and by understanding the "free associations," the uncensored and spontaneous thoughts of the patient, Freud attempted to arrive, with the patient, at knowing what the patient did not know before: his unconscious.

What were the theoretical premises for this use of the analysis of dreams and of free association for the discovery of the unconscious?

Doubtlessly in the first years of his psychoanalytic research, Freud shared the conventional rationalistic belief that knowledge was intellectual, theoretical knowledge. He thought that it was enough to explain to the patient why certain developments had taken place, and to tell him what the analyst had discovered in his unconscious. This intellectual knowledge, called "interpretation," was supposed to effect a change in the patient. But soon Freud and other analysts had to discover the truth of Spinoza's statement that *intellectual* knowledge is conducive to change only inasmuch as it is also *affective* knowledge. It became apparent that intellectual knowledge as such does not produce any change, except perhaps in the sense that by intellectual knowledge of his unconscious strivings a person may be better able to control them—which, however, is the aim of traditional ethics, rather than that of psychoanalysis. As long as the patient remains in the attitude of the detached self-observer, he is not in touch with his unconscious, except by *thinking* about it; he does not *experience* the wider, deeper reality within himself. Discovering one's unconscious is, precisely, *not* only an intellectual act, but also an affective experience, which can hardly be put into words, if at all. This does not mean that thinking and speculation may not precede the act of discovery; but the act of discovery is not an act of thinking but of *being aware* and, still better perhaps, simply of *seeing*. To be aware of experiences, thoughts or feelings which were unconscious, does not mean thinking *about* them, but *seeing* them, just as being aware of one's breathing does not mean to *think* about it. Awareness of the unconscious is an experience which is characterized by its spontaneity and suddenness. One's eyes are suddenly opened; oneself and the world appear in a different light, are seen from a different viewpoint. There is usually a good deal of anxiety aroused while the experience takes place, while afterward a new feeling of strength is present. The process of discovering the unconscious can be described as a series of ever-widening experiences, which are felt deeply and which transcend theoretical, intellectual knowledge.

In the question of the possibility of making the unconscious conscious, it is of the foremost importance to recognize factors which obstruct this process. There are many factors which make it difficult to arrive at insight into the unconscious. Such factors are mental rigidity, lack of proper orientation, hopelessness, lack of any possibility to change realistic conditions, etc. But there is probably no single factor which is more responsible for the difficulties of making the unconscious conscious than the mechanism which Freud called "resistance."

What is *resistance?* Like so many discoveries, it is so simple that one might say anyone could have discovered it—yet it required a great discoverer to recognize it. Let us take an example: your friend has to undertake a trip of which he is obviously afraid. You know that he is afraid, his wife knows it, everyone else knows it, but *he* does not know it. He claims one day that he does not feel well, the next day that there is no need to make the trip, the day after that that there are better ways to achieve the same result without traveling, then the next day that your persistence in reminding him of the trip is an attempt to force him, and since he does not want to be forced, he just won't make the trip, and so on, until he will say that it is now too late to go on the trip, anyway, hence there is no use in thinking any further about it. If, however, you mention to him, even in the most tactful way, that he might not want to go because he is afraid, you will get not a simple denial, but more likely a violent barrage of protestations and accusations which will eventually drive you into the role of having to apologize, or even—if *you* are now afraid of losing his friendship—of declaring that you never meant to say that he was afraid and, in fact, ending up with enthusiastic praise of his courage.

What has happened? The real motivation for not wanting to go is fear. (What he is afraid of is of no significance for the purposes of this discussion; suffice it to say, that his fear could be objectively justified or the reason for his fear merely imagined.) This fear is unconscious. Your friend, however, must choose a "reasonable" explanation for his not wanting to go—a "rationalization." He may discover every day a new one (anyone who has tried to give up smoking knows how easily rationalizations come) or stick to one main rationalization. It does not matter, in fact, whether the rationalization as such is valid or not; what matters is that it is not the effective or sufficient cause for his refusal to go. The most amazing fact, however, is the violence of his reaction when we mention the real motive to him, the intensity of his resistance. Should we not rather expect him to be glad, or even grateful for our remark, since it permits him to cope with the real motive for his reluctance? But whatever we think about what he should feel, the fact is that *he* does not feel it. Obviously he cannot bear the idea of being afraid. But why? There are several possibilities. Perhaps he has a narcissistic image of himself of which lack of fear is an integral part, and if this image is disturbed, his narcissistic self-admiration and, hence, his sense of his own value and his security would be threatened. Or perhaps his super-ego, the internalized code of right and wrong, happens to be such that fear or cowardice are bitterly condemned; hence to admit fear would mean to admit that he has acted against his code. Or, perhaps, he feels the need to save for his friends the picture of a man who is never frightened because he is so unsure of their friendship, that he is afraid they would cease liking him if they knew he was afraid. Any of these reasons may be effective, but *why* is it that they are so effective? One answer lies in the fact that his sense of identity is linked with these images. If they are not "true"—then who is he? What *is* true? Where does he stand in the world? Once these questions arise, the person feels deeply threatened. He has lost his familiar frame of orientation and with it his security. The anxiety aroused is not only a fear of something specific as Freud saw it, like a threat to the genitals, or to life, etc.; but it is also caused by the threat to one's identity. Resistance is an attempt to protect oneself from a fright which is comparable to the fright caused by even a small earthquake—nothing is secure, everything is shaky; I don't know who I am nor where I am. In fact, this experience feels like a small dose of insanity which for the moment, even though it may last only for seconds, feels more than uncomfortable.

More will be said later about resistance and the fears which produce repression, but we must first return to the discussion of some other aspects of the unconscious.

In psychoanalytic terminology, which by now has become quite popular, one speaks of "the unconscious" as if it were a place inside the person, like the cellar of a house. This idea has been reinforced by Freud's famous division of the personality into three parts: the Id, the

Ego, and the super-ego. The Id represents the sum total of instinctual desires, and at the same time, since most of them are not permitted to arrive at the level of awareness, it can be identified with the "unconscious." The Ego, representing man's organized personality inasmuch as it observes reality and has the function of realistic appreciation, at least as far as survival is concerned, may be said to represent "consciousness." The super-ego, the internalization of father's (and society's) commands and prohibitions, can be both conscious and unconscious, and hence does not lend itself to being identified with the unconscious or the conscious respectively. The topographical use of the unconscious has certainly been stimulated further by the general tendency in our time to think in terms of *having,* which will be discussed later on in this chapter. People say that they *have* insomnia, instead of *being* sleepless, or of *having* a problem of depression, rather than of *being* depressed; thus they *have* a car, a house, a child, as they have a problem, a feeling, a psychoanalyst—and an unconscious.

This is the reason why so many people today prefer to speak of the "subconscious"; it is still more clearly a region, rather than a function; while I can say I am unconscious of this or that, one could not say, "I am subconscious of it." [1] Another difficulty in the Freudian concept of the unconscious lies in the fact that it tends to identify a certain *content,* the instinctual strivings of the Id, with a certain *state of awareness/unawareness,* the unconscious, although Freud was careful to keep the concept

---

[1] Jung's use of the term "unconscious" has not helped to discourage the topographical usage of this concept. While for Freud the unconscious is the cellar full of vices, Jung's unconscious is rather a cave filled with man's original but forgotten treasures of wisdom (although not exclusively so), laid over by intellectualizations.

of the unconscious separate from that of the Id. One must not lose sight of the fact that one is dealing here with two entirely distinct concepts; one deals with certain instinctual impulses—another with a certain state of perception—unawareness or awareness. It so happens that the average person in our society is unaware of certain instinctual needs. But the cannibal is quite aware of his desire to incorporate another human being, the psychotic is quite aware of that or other archaic desires, and so are most of us in our dreams. It will clarify the understanding of "the" unconscious if we insist on the separation between the concept of archaic contents and that of the state of unawareness, or unconsciousness.

The term "the unconscious" is actually a mystification (even though one might use it for reasons of convenience, as I am guilty of doing in these pages). There is no such thing as *the* unconscious; there are only experiences of which we are aware, and others of which we are not aware, that is, *of which we are unconscious.* If I hate a man because I am afraid of him, and if I am aware of my hate but not of my fear, we may say that my hate is conscious and that my fear is unconscious; still, my fear does not lie in that mysterious place: "the" unconscious.

But we repress not only sexual impulses or affects such as hate and fear; we repress also the awareness of facts provided they contradict certain ideas and interests which we do not want to have threatened. Good examples for this kind of repression are offered in the field of international relations. We find here a great deal of simple repression of factual knowledge. The average man, and even policy makers, forget conveniently facts which do not fit into their political reasoning. For instance, while discussing the Berlin question in the spring of 1961 with a very intelligent and knowledgeable newspaperman, I mentioned the fact that in my opinion we had given

. Khrushchev reason to believe that we were willing to compromise on the Berlin question in terms which had been
dealt with in the Foreign Ministers' conference in Geneva
in 1959, those of symbolic troop reduction and cessation of
anticommunist propaganda from West Berlin. The newspaperman insisted that there had been no such conference, and that there was never a discussion of such terms.
He had completely repressed the awareness of facts which
he had known less than two years before. Not always is
the repression as drastic as it was in this case. More frequent than the repression of a well-known fact is the repression of the "potentially known" fact. An example for
this mechanism is the phenomenon that millions of Germans, including many leading politicians and generals,
claimed not to have known of the worst Nazi atrocities.
The average American was (I say "was" because at the
time of this writing the Germans are our closest allies,
and hence all these things are looked at in a different way than they were at the time when the Germans
were still "the enemy") prone to say that they must be
lying, since they hardly could have helped seeing the
facts in front of their eyes. Those who said this forgot,
however, man's capacity of not observing what he does
not want to observe; hence, that he may be sincere in
denying a knowledge which he would have, if he wanted
only to have it. (H. S. Sullivan coined the very appropriate
term "selective inattention" for this phenomenon.) Another form of repression lies in remembering certain aspects of an event and not others. When one speaks today
of the "appeasement" of the thirties, one remembers that
England and France, being afraid of a rearmed Germany,
tried to satisfy Hitler's demands, hoping that these concessions would induce him not to demand more. What is
forgotten, however, is that the conservative government in
England under Baldwin as well as that under Chamber-

lain, was sympathetic to Nazi Germany as well as to Mussolini's Italy. Had it not been for these sympathies, one
could have stopped Germany's military development long
before there was any need for appeasement; official indig-
nation with Nazi ideology was the result of the political
rift, and not its cause. Still another form of repression is the
one in which not the fact is repressed but its emotional
and moral significance. In a war, for instance, cruelties
committed by the enemy are experienced as just another
proof of his devilish viciousness; the same or similar acts
committed by one's own side are felt to be regrettable
though understandable reactions; not to speak of the many
who will find the enemy's actions devilish, and the same
actions, when performed on their own side, not even regrettable but perfectly justified.

To sum up: the center of Freud's thought was that
man's *subjectivity* is, in fact, determined by *objective* factors—objective as far as man's own consciousness is concerned—which act behind man's back, as it were, determining his thoughts and feelings, and thus indirectly his
actions. Man, so proud of his freedom to think and to
choose is, in fact, a marionette moved by strings behind
and above him which in turn are directed by forces unknown to his consciousness. In order to give himself the
illusion that he acts according to his own free will, man
invents rationalizations which make it appear as if he
does what he has to do because he has chosen to do so for
rational or moral reasons. But Freud did not end on a
note of fatalism confirming man's utter helplessness against
the powers which determine him. He postulated that man
can become aware of the very forces which act behind his
back—and that in becoming aware of them he enlarges
the realm of freedom and is able to transform himself from
a helpless puppet moved by unconscious forces to a self-
aware and free man who determines his own destiny.

Freud expressed this aim in the words, "Where there is Id there shall be Ego."

The concept of unconscious forces determining man's consciousness, and the choices he makes, have a tradition in Western thought going back to the seventeenth century. The first thinker who had a clear concept of the unconscious was Spinoza. He assumed that men "are conscious of their own desire, but are ignorant of the causes whereby that desire has been determined." In other words, the average man is not free, but he lives under the illusion of being free because he is motivated by factors unconscious to him. For Spinoza this very existence of unconscious motivation constitutes human bondage. But he did not leave it at that. The attainment of freedom, for Spinoza, was based on an ever-increasing awareness of the reality inside and outside of man.

The idea of unconscious motivation was expressed in a very different context by A. Smith, who wrote that economic man "is led by an invisible hand to promote an end which was no part of his intention." [1]

Again in a different context we find the concept of the unconscious in Nietzsche's famous saying: "My memory says I have done this. My pride says I have not done it; my memory yields."

Actually the whole trend of thought which was concerned with uncovering the objective factors determining human consciousness and behavior is to be looked upon as part of the general trend to grasp reality rationally and scientifically, which has characterized Western thought

---

[1] A. Smith, *An Inquiry into the Nature and Causes of the Wealth of Nations*, The Modern Library, New York, 1937, p. 423. This quote as well as the suggestion of A. Smith's role in the development of the concept of the unconscious I owe to Robert Tucker's excellent analysis of this problem in *Philosophy and Myth of Karl Marx*, Cambridge University Press, Cambridge, 1961, p. 66.

since the end of the Middle Ages. The medieval world had been well ordered and seemed to be secure. Man had been created by God and was watched over by him; man's world was the center of the universe; man's consciousness was the last mental, indubitable entity, just as the atom was the smallest, indivisible physical entity. Within a few hundred years this world broke to pieces. The earth ceased to be the center of the universe, man was the product of an evolutionary development starting with the most primitive forms of life, the physical world transcended all concepts of time and space which had seemed to be secure even a generation before, and consciousness was recognized as an instrument for hiding thought, rather than being the bastion of truth.

The writer who made the most significant contribution to the overthrow of the dominant position of consciousness, aside from Spinoza before him and Freud after him, was Marx. He was probably influenced by Spinoza, whose *Ethics* he had studied thoroughly. More importantly, Hegel's philosophy of history had a decisive influence on Marx's thought and contained the concept of man serving the aims of history without his own knowledge. According to Hegel it is the "cunning of reason" (die List der Vernunft") which makes man an agent of the absolute idea while he is subjectively driven by his own conscious goals and individual passions. The individual man and his consciousness, in Hegel's philosophy is the marionette on the stage of history while the Idea (or God) pulls the strings.

Marx, descending from the heaven of Hegel's Idea to the earth of human activity, was able to give a much more concrete and precise expression to the idea of the function of human consciousness and the objective factors influencing it.

In the *German Ideology* Marx wrote: "Not consciousness

determines life but life determines consciousness," and
in this difference he sees the decisive difference between
Hegel's and his own thinking. "It is not the consciousness
of men," Marx wrote later, "that determines his existence,
but on the contrary, it is their social existence that determines consciousness." [1] While man believes that his
thoughts mold his social existence, the facts are the re-
verse: his social reality molds his thought. "The production
of ideas," wrote Marx, "of conceptions, of consciousness, is at first directly interwoven with the material activity and the material intercourse of men, the language of
real life. Conceiving, thinking, the mental intercourse of
men, appear at this stage as the direct efflux from their material behavior. The same applies to mental production as
expressed in the language of politics, laws, morality, religion, metaphysics of a people. Men are the producers of
their conceptions, ideas, etc.—real, active men, as they
are conditioned by the definite development of their productive forces and of the intercourse corresponding to
these, up to its furthest forms. Consciousness can never
be anything else than conscious existence, and the existence of men is their actual life-process. If in all ideology
men and their circumstances appear upside down as in a
*camera obscura,** this phenomenon arises just as much
from their historical life-process as the inversion of objects
on the retina does from their physical life-process." [2]
More specifically, applying Hegel's theories of the "cunning of reason" to his concept of social classes, Marx stated

---

[1] *Preface to a Contribution to the Critique of Political Economy.*

* An instrument perfected in the late Middle Ages, to throw by
means of mirrors an image of a scene on a plane surface. It was
widely used by artists to establish the correct proportions of a
natural object or scene. The image appeared on the paper in-
verted, though the later use of a lens corrected this.

[2] *German Ideology,* pp. 13-4.

in the German Ideology that the class achieves an independent existence over and against individuals whose existence and personal development are predetermined by their class.

Marx observed the connection between consciousness and language and emphasized the social nature of consciousness: "Language is as old as consciousness, language is practical consciousness, as it exists for other men, and for that reason is really beginning to exist for me personally as well; for language, like consciousness, only arises from the need, the necessity of intercourse with other men. Where there exists a relationship, it exists for me: the animal has no 'relations' with anything, cannot have any. For the animal, its relation to others does not exist as a relation. Consciousness is therefore from the very beginning a social product, and remains so as long as men exist at all. Consciousness is at first, of course, merely consciousness concerning the immediate sensuous environment and consciousness of the limited connection with other persons and things outside the individual who is growing self-conscious. At the same time it is consciousness of nature, which first appears to man as a completely alien, all-powerful, and unassailable force, with which men's relations are purely animal and by which they are overawed like beasts; it is thus a purely animal consciousness of nature [natural religion]." [1]

While Marx already used the term *"repression* (Verdraengung) of the ordinary natural desires" in the *German Ideology*,[2] Rosa Luxemburg, one of the most bril-

---

[1] *German Ideology*, p. 19.
[2] MEGA I, 5, p. 423. I am grateful to Maximilien Rubel for calling my attention to this sentence. Rubel quotes the passage in his Karl Marx, *Essai de Biographie Intellectuelle*, Librairie Marcel Riviere et Cie., Paris 1957, p. 225. Rubel makes in the same context some very interesting remarks on the connection between Marx's theory and psychoanalytic thinking.

liant Marxists in the pre-1914 period, expressed the
Marxist theory of the determining effect of historical process on man in straight psychoanalytic terminology. "The
unconscious," she wrote, "comes before the conscious.
The logic of the historic process comes before the subjective logic of the human beings who participate in the
historic process." [1] This formulation expresses the Marxian
thought in full clarity. Man's consciousness, that is, his
"subjective process," is determined by "the logic of the
historic process," which R. Luxemburg equates with
the "unconscious."

At this point the Freudian and the Marxian "unconscious" may seem not to denote more than a common
word. Only if we pursue Marx's ideas on this problem
further shall we discover that there is more common
ground in their respective theories, even though they are
by no means identical.

Marx has given a good deal of thought to the role of
consciousness in the life of the individual in a passage
which precedes the one just quoted where he uses the
word "repression." He speaks about the fact that it is
nonsense if one believes "that one could satisfy one passion, separate it from all the others, without satisfying
oneself, the whole living individual. If this passion assumes an abstract, separate character, hence if the satisfaction of the individual occurs as the satisfaction of a
single passion . . . the reason is not to be found in *consciousness*, but in *being*; not in thinking, but in living; it is
to be found in the empirical development and self-expres-

---

[1] Rosa Luxemburg, *Leninism or Marxism* (first published in 1904
in the Russian *Iskra* and the German *Neue Zeit* under the original
title of *Organizational Questions of the Russian Social Democracy*)
recently published *The Russian Revolution and Leninism or Marxism?* Ann Arbor, Mich.: the University of Michigan Press, 1961,
p. 93.

sion of the individual, which, in turn, depends on the conditions of the world in which he lives. (die wiederum von der Weltverhältnissen abhängt.)" [1] In this passage Marx establishes the polarity between thinking and living which is parallel to that between consciousness and being. The social constellation of which he spoke before molds, so he says here, the being of the individual and thus, indirectly, his thinking. (The passage also is interesting because Marx develops here a most significant idea on a problem of psychopathology. If man satisfies only one alienated passion, he, the total man, remains unsatisfied; he is, as we would say today, neurotic, precisely because of the fact that he has become the slave of the one alienated passion and has lost the experience of himself as a total and alive person.) Marx, like Freud, believed that man's consciousness is mostly "false consciousness." Man believes that his thoughts are authentic and the product of *his* thinking activity while they are in reality determined by the objective forces which work behind his back; in Freud's theory these objective forces represent physiological and biological needs, in Marx's theory they represent the social and economic historical forces which determine the being and thus indirectly the consciousness of the individual.

Let us think of an example: The industrial method of production as it has developed in the last decades is based on the existence of large centralized enterprises which are controlled by a managerial elite, and in which hundreds of thousands of workers and clerks work together, smoothly and without friction. This bureaucratic industrial system shapes the character of the bureaucrats as well as that of the workers. It also shapes their thoughts. The bureaucrat is conservative and adverse to taking risks. His

---

[1] MEGA I, 5, p. 242 (My translation, E.F.).

main desire is to advance, and he can best do so by avoiding risky decisions and by allowing himself to be led by the interest in the proper functioning of the organization as his guiding principle. The workers and clerks, on their side, tend to feel satisfied in being a part of the Organization provided their material and psychological rewards are sufficient to justify this. Their own trade union organizations resemble in many ways that of their industry: large-scale organizations, bureaucratic and well-paid leadership, little active participation of the individual member. The development of large-scale industry is accompanied by the development of large-scale centralized government and armed services, both of which follow the same principles which guide the industrial corporations.[1] This type of social organization leads to the formation of elites, the business, government, and miltary elites and, to a degree, to the trade union elites. The business, government, and military elites are closely interwoven in personnel, in attitudes, and in ways of thinking. In spite of the political and social differences between the "capitalist" countries and the "communist" Soviet Union, the way of feeling and thinking among their respective elites is similar, precisely because the basic mode of production is similar. [2]

---

[1] It is an ironical fact that those conservatives who are opposed to big government (or at least pretend to be) are usually not opposed to big business or to big military establishments.

[2] C. Wright Mills called these elites *"The Power Elite"* and analyzed them in a masterful book of this title. He did not however, fully recognize that these power elites are the product of a specific way of production and social organization and, hence, that their existence confirms the basic Marxian assumption, rather than contradicts it. In his last brilliant book, *"The Marxists"* (Dell Publishing Corporation, New York, 1962), he criticizes Marxist economic determinism and suggests that military and political determinism are equally valid assumptions (p. 126). I believe these elites and their role can be best understood precisely from the standpoint of the Marxian model.

The consciousness of the members of the elites is a product of their social existence. They consider their way of organization and the values that are implied in it as being in "the best interests of man," they have a picture of human nature which makes this assumption plausible, they are hostile to any idea or system which questions or endangers their own system; they are against disarmament if they feel that their organizations are threatened by it, they are suspicious and hostile of a system in which their class has been replaced by a different and new class of managers. Consciously they honestly believe that they are motivated by patriotic concern for their country, duty, moral and political principles, and so on. The elites on both sides are equally caught in thoughts and ideas which follow from the nature of their mode of production and they are both sincere in their conscious thoughts. Precisely because they are sincere, and because they are not aware of the real motivations behind their thoughts, it is difficult for them to change their minds. These people are not driven by an overwhelming greed for power, money, or prestige. To be sure, such motives exist too; but the people in whom this is the all-consuming motive are the exception rather than the rule. Personally the members of all the elites would be just as willing to make sacrifices and to renounce certain advantages as anybody else. The motivating factor is that their social function forms their consciousness, and hence their conviction that they are right, that their aims are justified and, in fact, beyond doubt. This explains also another and very puzzling phenomenon. We see that the elites of the two great blocs are on a collision course and that there are great difficulties in coming to an arrangement which will secure peace. There is no doubt that nuclear war would mean the death of most members of the elites, of most of their families, and the destruction of most of their organizations. If they were driven mainly by lust for money and power, how could one understand that this greed would not yield to the fear of death, except in the case of exceptionally neurotic individuals? The point lies precisely in the difficulty to change their viewpoint. Because to them, theirs is the rational, decent, honorable way of thinking—and if the nuclear holocaust will destroy everybody—it cannot be helped since there is no other course of action besides that of "reason," "decency," and "honor."

Thus far I have tried to show how in Marx's thought social existence determines consciousness. But Marx was not a "determinist," as it often is stated. His position is very much the same as Spinoza's: we are determined by forces outside of our conscious selves, and by passions and interests which direct us behind our backs. Inasmuch as this is the case, we are not free. *But* we can emerge from this bondage and enlarge the realm of freedom by becoming fully aware of reality, and hence of necessity, by giving up illusions, and by transforming ourselves from somnabulistic, unfree, determined, dependent, passive persons into awakened, aware, active, independent ones. Both for Spinoza and for Marx the aim of life is liberation from bondage, and the way to this aim is the overcoming of illusions and the full use of our active powers. Freud's position is essentially the same; he spoke less of freedom versus bondage than of mental health versus mental sickness. He, too, saw that man is determined by objective factors (the libido and its fate) but he thought that man can overcome this determination by overcoming his illusions, by waking up to reality, and by becoming aware of what is real but unconscious. Freud's principle as a therapist was that awareness of the unconscious is the way to the cure of mental illness. As a social philosopher he believed in the same principle: only if we become aware of reality and overcome our illusions can we attain the optimal strength to cope with life. Freud expressed these ideas perhaps most explicitly in *The Future of an Illusion.* "Perhaps," he wrote, "those who do not suffer from the neurosis will need no intoxicant to deaden it. They will, it is true, find themselves in a difficult situation. They will have to admit to themselves the full extent of their helplessness and their insignificance in the machinery of the universe; they can no longer be the center of creation, no longer the object of tender care on the part of a beneficent Providence. They will be in the same position as a child who has left the parental house where he was so warm and comfortable. But surely infantilism is destined to be surmounted. Men cannot remain children forever; they must in the end go out into 'hostile life.' We may call this *'education to reality.'* " [1] And further: "Our God, Logos, is perhaps not a very almighty one, and he may only be able to fulfill a small part of what his predecessors have promised. If we have to acknowledge this we shall accept it with resignation. We shall not on that account lose our interest in the world and in life . . . no, our science is no illusion. But an illusion it would be to suppose that what science cannot give us we can get elsewhere." [2]

For Marx, awareness of illusions is the condition for freedom and human action. He expressed this idea brilliantly in his early writings, in the context of his analysis of the function of religion: *"Religious* distress is at the

---

[1] S. Freud, *The Future of an Illusion,* The Standard Edition of the Complete Psychological Works of Sigmund Freud, The Hogarth Press, London, 1961, Vol. XXI, p. 49.

[2] *Ibid.,* pp. 54-6.

same time the *expression* of real distress and the *protest* against real distress. Religion is the sigh of the oppressed creature, the heart of a heartless world, just as it is the spirit of an unspiritual situation. It is the *opium* of the people.

"The abolition of religion as the *illusory* happiness of the people is required for their *real* happiness. The demand to give up the illusions about its condition is the *demand to give up a condition which needs illusions*. The criticism of religion is therefore *in embryo the criticism of the vale of woe, the halo* of which is religion.

"Criticism has plucked the imaginary flowers from the chain not so that man will wear the chain without any fantasy or consolation, but so that he will shake off the chain and cull the living flower. The criticism of religion disillusions man, to make him think and act and shape his reality like a man who has been disillusioned and has come to reason, so that he will revolve round himself and therefore round his true sun. Religion is only the illusory sun, which revolves round man as long as he does not revolve round himself." [1]

How can man attain the goal of freeing himself from illusions? Marx thought his goal could be achieved by *reform of consciousness*. "The *reform of consciousness* consists exclusively in the fact that one lets the world become aware of its consciousness, that one awakens the world from the dream it is dreaming about itself, that one *interprets* its own actions to the world . . . our motto must be: reform of consciousness, not through dogmas

---

[1] From *Toward the Critique of Hegel's Philosophy of Right* (Zur Kritik der Hegelschen Rechtsphilosophy, MEGA I, 1, pp. 607-8). Translation quoted from Lewis S. Feuer, *Marx & Engels*, a Doubleday Anchor Original, New York, 1959, p. 263.

but by analyzing the mystical self-confused consciousness, whether it has a political or a religious content. One
will see, then, that the world has possessed already for
a long time the dream of something, of which it must
only have consciousness in order to possess it in reality.
One will see that we are not dealing with a big hiatus
between past and present but with the *realization* (Voll-
ziehung) of the thoughts of the past. Eventually one will
see that mankind does not begin any new task but ac-
complishes its old task with consciousness . . . this is a
confession, nothing else. In order to have its sins for-
given, mankind has only to explain them for what they
are." [1]

To sum up this confrontation between Marx's and
Freud's concept of the unconscious: both believe that
most of what man thinks consciously is determined by
forces which operate behind his back, that is, without man's
knowledge; that man explains his actions to himself as
being rational or moral and these rationalizations (false
consciousness, ideology) satisfy him subjectively. But
being driven by forces unknown to him, man is not free.
He can attain freedom (and health) only by becoming
aware of these motivating forces, that is of reality, and
thus he can become the master of his life (within the
limitations of reality) rather than the slave of blind forces.
The fundamental difference between Marx and Freud
lies in their respective concept of the nature of these forces
determining man. For Freud they are essentially physiological (libido) or biological (death instinct and life instinct). For Marx they are the historical forces which pass
through an evolution in the process of man's socio-
economic development. For Marx man's consciousness is
determined by his being, his being by his practice of life,

---

[1] K. Marx, *Letter to R.,* September 1843, MEGA I, 1, p. 575
(My translation, E.F.).

his practice of life by his mode of producing his livelihood, that is, by his mode of production and the social
structure, mode of distribution and consumption resulting
from it.[1]

Marx's and Freud's concepts are not mutually exclusive. This is so precisely because Marx sets out from the
real active men and on the basis of their real life-process,
including, of course, their biological and physiological
conditions. Marx recognized the sexual drive as one existing under all circumstances which can be changed by
social conditions only as far as form and direction are
concerned.

Yet while the Freudian theory might be incorporated
in some fashion into that of Marx, there remain two fundamental differences. For Marx, man's being and his consciousness are determined by the structure of the society
of which he is a part; for Freud, society only influences
his being by greater or lesser repression of his innate physiological and biological equipment. From this first difference follows the second: Freud believed that man can
overcome repression without social changes. Marx on the
other hand was the first thinker who saw that the realization of the universal and fully awakened man can occur
only together with social changes which lead to a new and
truly human economic and social organization of mankind.

Marx has only stated in general terms his theory of the
determination of consciousness by social forces. In the fol-

---

[1] Karl Manheim was the first to point out that the socialist doctrine possessed "new intellectual weapons" in the capacity of the
"unmasking of the unconscious" (their opponents'). He also saw
that the "collective unconscious and the activity impelled by it
serve to disguise certain aspects of social reality . . ." (Karl
Manheim, *Ideology and Utopia,* a Harvest Book, Harcourt, Brace
and Co. New York, p. 33ff.)

lowing I try to show how this determination operates concretely and specifically.[1]

For any experience to come into awareness, it must be comprehensible in accordance with the categories in which conscious thought is organized. I can become aware of any occurrence, inside or outside of myself, only when it can be linked with the system of categories in which I perceive. Some of the categories, such as time and space, may be universal, and may constitute categories of perception common to all men. Others, such as causality, may be a valid category for many, but not for all forms of conscious perception. Other categories are even less gen-

---

[1] Since there are certain similarities between the concepts used here and those used by Jung, a word of explanation seems indicated. First of all it should be mentioned that Jung emphasizes the social character of neurosis more than Freud did. He believed that "neuroses are in most cases not just private concerns but social phenomena . . ." He furthermore held that underneath the personal unconscious is a deeper layer, the "collective unconscious," which "is not individual but universal; in contrast to the personal psyche it has contents and mores of behavior that are more or less the same everywhere and in all individuals. It is, in other words, identical in all men and thus constitutes a common psychic substitute of a superpersonal nature which is present in every one of us." I agree with Jung in the very central issue of the universal character of the psychic substance present in every one of us. The difference between Jung's term "collective unconscious" and the "social unconscious" as employed here is this: "collective unconscious" directly denotes the universal psyche, much of which cannot even become conscious. The concept of the social unconscious starts out with the notion of the repressive character of society and refers to that specific part of human experience which a given society does not permit to reach awareness; it is that part of humanity in man which his society has estranged from him; the social unconscious is the socially repressed part of the universal psyche.

eral and differ from culture to culture. For instance, in a pre-industrial culture people may not perceive certain things in terms of their commercial value, while they do so in an industrial system. However this may be, experience can enter into awareness only under the condition that it can be perceived, related, and ordered in terms of a conceptual system [1] and of its categories. This system is in itself a result of social evolution. Every society, by its own practice of living and by the mode of relatedness, of feeling and perceiving, develops a system, or categories, which determines the forms of awareness. This system works, as it were, like a *socially conditioned filter:* experience cannot enter awareness unless it can penetrate this filter.[2]

The question, then, is to understand more concretely how this "social filter" operates, and how it happens that it permits certain experiences to be filtered through while others are stopped from entering awareness.

---

[1] The same idea was first expressed by E. Schachtel (in an illuminating paper on "Memory and Childhood Amnesia," in *Psychiatry,* Vol. X, No. 1, 1947) with regard to the amnesia of childhood memories. As the title indicates, he is concerned there with the more specific problem of childhood amnesia, and with the difference between the categories ("schematas") employed by the child and those employed by the adult. He concludes that "the incompatibility of early childhood experience with the categories and organization of adult memory is to a large extent due to . . . the conventionalization of the adult memory." In my opinion, what he says about childhood and adult memory holds true, but we find not only the differences between childhood and adult categories, but also those between various cultures and, furthermore, the problem is not only that of memory, but also that of consciousness in general.

[2] In the following I have drawn on my discussion of thtis subject in *"Zen Buddhism and Psychoanalysis"* by D. T. Suzuki, E. Fromm, R. de Martino, Harper Bros., New York, 1960.

First of all, we must consider that many experiences do not lend themselves easily to being perceived in awareness. Pain is perhaps the physical experience which best lends itself to being consciously perceived; sexual desire, hunger, etc., also are easily perceived; quite obviously, all sensations which are relevant to individual or group survival have easy access to awareness. But when it comes to a more subtle or complex experience, like *"seeing a rosebud in the early morning, a drop of dew on it, while the air is still chilly, the sun coming up, a bird singing"*— this is an experience which, in some cultures, easily lends itself to awareness (for instance, in Japan), while in modern Western culture this same experience will usually not come into awareness because it is not sufficiently "important" or "eventful" to be noticed. Whether or not subtle effective experiences can arrive at awareness depends on the degree to which such experiences are cultivated in a given culture. There are many affective experiences for which a given language has no word, while another language may be rich in words which express these feelings. In a language in which different affective experiences are not expressed by different words, it is almost impossible for one's experiences to come to clear awareness. Generally speaking, it may be said that an experience rarely comes into awareness for which the language has no word.

This fact is of special relevance with regard to such experiences which do not fit into our intellectual rational scheme of things. In English, for instance, the word "awe" (like in Hebrew "nora") means two different things. Awe is the feeling of intense fright as it is still indicated in "awful": and awe also means something like intense admiration, as we still find it in awesome (and in awed by). From a standpoint of conscious rational thought, fright and admiration are distinct feelings, hence they cannot be denoted by the same word; and if there is one word like awe, it is used in the one *or* the other sense, and the fact is forgotten that it actually means fright *and* admiration. In our *feeling* experience, however, fright and admiration are by no means mutually exclusive. On the contrary, as a visceral experience, fear and admiration are frequently part of one complex feeling, which, however, modern man is usually not aware of as such. It seems that the language of peoples who emphasized less than we do the intellectual aspect of experience, has more words which expressed the feeling as such, while our modern languages tend to express only such feelings which can stand the test of our kind of logic. Incidentally, this phenomenon constitutes one of the greatest difficulties for dynamic psychology. Our language just does not give us the words which we need to describe many visceral experiences which do not fit our scheme of thoughts. Hence psychoanalysis has really no adequate language at its disposal. It could do what some other sciences have done and use symbols to denote certain complex feelings. For instance, $\frac{a}{t}$ could stand for that complex feeling of admiration and terror which was once expressed by one word. Or xy could stand for the feeling of "aggressive defiance, superiority, accusation $+$ hurt innocence, martyrdom, being persecuted and falsely accused." Again, this latter feeling is not a synthesis of different feelings, as our language would make us believe, but one specific feeling which can be observed in oneself and in others once one transcends the barrier of the assumption, that nothing can be felt which cannot be "thought." If one does not use abstract symbols, the most adequate, paradoxically enough, scientific language for psychoanalysis is actually that of symbolism, poetry or reference to themes of mythology. (Freud often chose the latter way.)

But if the psychoanalyst thinks he can be scientific by using technical terms of our language to denote emotional phenomena, he deceives himself and speaks of abstract constructs which do not correspond to the reality of felt experience.

But this is only one aspect of the filtering function of language. Different languages differ not only by the fact that they vary in the diversity of words they use to denote certain affective experiences, but also by their syntax, their grammar, and the root-meaning of their words. The whole language contains an attitude of life, is a frozen expression of experiencing life in a certain way.[1]

Here are a few examples. There are languages in which the verb form "it rains," for instance, is conjugated differently depending on whether I say that it rains because I have been out in the rain and have got wet, or because I have seen it raining from the inside of a hut, or because somebody has told me that it rains. It is quite obvious that the emphasis of the language on these different *sources* of experiencing a fact (in this case, that it rains) has a deep influence on *the way* people experience facts. (In our modern culture, for instance, with its emphasis on the purely intellectual side of knowledge, it makes little difference how I know a fact, whether from direct or indirect experience, or from hearsay.) Or, in Hebrew, the main principle of conjugation is to determine whether an activity is complete (perfect) or incomplete (imperfect), while the time in which it occurs—past, present, future— is expressed only in a secondary fashion. In Latin both principles (time and perfection) are used together, while

---

[1] Cf. the pathfinding contribution of Benjamin Whorf in his *Collected Papers on Metalinguistics* (Washington, D.C.: Foreign Service Institute, 1952).

in English we are predominantly oriented in the sense of time. Again it goes without saying that this difference in conjugation expresses a difference in experiencing.[1]

Still another example is to be found in the different uses of verbs and nouns in various languages, or even among different people speaking the same language. The noun refers to a "thing"; the verb refers to an activity. An increasing number of people prefer to think in terms of *having things,* instead of *being* or *acting;* hence, they prefer nouns to verbs.

Language, by its words, its grammar, its syntax, by the whole spirit which is frozen in it, determines which experiences penetrate to our awareness.

The second aspect of the filter which makes awareness possible is the *logic* which directs the thinking of people in a given culture. Just as most people assume that their language is "natural" and that other languages only use different words for the same things, they assume also that the rules which determine proper thinking are natural and universal ones; that what is illogical in one cultural system is illogical in any other because it conflicts with "natural" logic. A good example of this is the difference between Aristotelian and paradoxical logic.

Aristotelian logic is based on the law of identity which states that A is A, the law of contradiction (A is not non-A), and the law of the excluded middle (A cannot be A *and* non-A, neither A *nor* non-A). Aristotle stated it: "It is impossible for the same thing at the same time to belong and not to belong to the same thing in the same

---

[1] The significance of this difference becomes quite apparent in the English and German translations of the Old Testament. Often when the Hebrew text uses the perfect tense for an emotional experience like loving, meaning, "I love fully," the translator misunderstands and writes, "I loved."

respect. . . . This, then, is the most certain of all principles." [1]

In opposition to Aristotelian logic is what one might call *paradoxical logic,* which assumes that A and non-A do not exclude each other as predicates of X. Paradoxical logic was predominant in Chinese and Indian thinking, in Heraclitus' philosophy, and then again under the name of dialectics in the thought of Hegel and Marx. The general principle of paradoxical logic has been clearly described in general terms by Lao-tse: "Words that are strictly true seem to be paradoxical." [2] And by Chuang-tzu: "That which is one is one. That which is not-one, is also one."

Inasmuch as a person lives in a culture in which the correctness of Aristotelian logic is not doubted, it is exceedingly difficult, if not impossible, for him to be aware of experiences which contradict Aristotelian logic, hence which from the standpoint of his culture are nonsensical. A good example is Freud's concept of ambivalence, which says that one can experience love and hate for the same person at the same time. This experience, which from the standpoint of paradoxical logic is quite "logical," does not make sense from the standpoint of Aristotelian logic. As a result it is exceedingly difficult for most people to be aware of feelings of ambivalence. If they are aware of love, they cannot be aware of hate—since it would be utterly nonsensical to have two contradictory feelings at the same time toward the same person. [3]

---

[1] Aristotle, *Metaphysics,* Book Gamma, 1005b 20. Quoted from Aristotle's *Metaphysics,* translated by R. Hope (New York: Columbia University Press, 1952).

[2] Lao-tse, *The Tâo Teh King, The Sacred Books of the East,* ed. by F. Max Mueller, Vol. XXXIX (London: Oxford University Press, 1927), p. 120.

[3] Cf. my more detailed discussion of this problem in *The Art of Loving,* World Perspective Series (New York: Harper & Brothers, 1956) p. 72ff.

While language and logic are parts of the social filter which makes it difficult or impossible for an experience to enter awareness, the third part of the social filter is the most important one for it is the one that does not *permit* certain feelings to reach consciousness and tends to expel them from this realm if they have reached it. It is made up by the social taboos which declare certain ideas and feelings to be improper, forbidden, dangerous, and which prevent them from even reaching the level of consciousness.

An example taken from a primitive tribe may serve as an introduction to the problem indicated here. In a tribe of warriors, for instance, whose members live by killing and robbing the members of other tribes, there might be an individual who feels a revulsion against killing and robbing. Yet it is most unlikely that he will be aware of this feeling since it would be incompatible with that of the whole tribe; to be aware of this incompatible feeling would mean the danger of being completely isolated and ostracized. Hence an individual with such an experience of revulsion would probably develop a psychosomatic symptom such as vomiting, instead of letting the feeling of revulsion penetrate to his awareness. Exactly the contrary would be found in the case of a member of a peaceful agricultural tribe who has the impulse to go out and kill and rob members of other groups. He also would probably not permit himself to become aware of his impulses, but instead would develop a symptom—maybe intense fright.

Still another example, one from our own civilization: there must be many shopkeepers in our big cities who have a customer who badly needs, let us say, a suit of clothes, but who does not have sufficient money to buy even the cheapest one. Among those shopkeepers (especially the well-to-do ones) there must be a few who would have the natural human impulse to give the suit to the customer for the price that he can pay. But how many will permit themselves to be aware of such an impulse? I assume very few. The majority will repress it, and we might find among them quite a few who will have a dream during the following night which might express the repressed impulse in one form or another.

Another example: the modern "organization man" might feel that his life makes little sense, that he is bored by what he is doing, that he has little freedom to do and think as he sees fit, that he is chasing after an illusion of happiness which never comes true. But if he were aware of such feelings, he would be greatly hindered in his proper social functioning. Hence such awareness would constitute a real danger to society as it is organized; and as a result, the feeling is repressed.

Or, there must be many people who sense that it is irrational to buy a new car every two years and who might even have a feeling of sadness when they have to part from a car they have been using, one that has "grown on them." Yet if many were aware of such feelings, there would be danger that they would act on them— and where would our economy be, which is based on relentless consumption? Then again, is it possible that most people should be so lacking in natural intelligence that they do not see with how much incompetence many of their leaders—whatever the method by which they came to the top—perform their functions? Yet where would social cohesion and unified action be if such facts became conscious to more than a tiny minority? Is reality in this respect any different from what happens in Andersen's fairy tale of the emperor without clothes? Although the emperor is naked, only a little boy perceives this fact, while the rest of the people are convinced that the emperor is wearing beautiful clothes.

The irrationalities of any given society result in the necessity for its members to repress the awareness of many of their own feelings and observations. This necessity is the greater in proportion to the extent to which a society is not representative of all its members. Greek society did not pretend to fulfill the interests of all its people. The slaves, even according to Aristotle, were not full-fledged human beings; hence neither the citizens nor the slaves had to repress much in this respect. But for societies which pretend to care for the welfare of all, this problem does exist if they fail to do so. Throughout human history, with the exception, perhaps, of some primitive societies, the table has always been set only for a few, and the vast majority received nothing but the remaining crumbs. If the majority had been fully aware of the fact that they were being cheated, a resentment might have developed which would have endangered the existing order. Hence such thoughts had to be repressed and those in whom this process of repression did not take place adequately were in danger of their lives or freedom.

The most revolutionary change in our times lies in the fact that all the peoples of the world have opened their eyes and are aware of their desire for a dignified material life, and that man has discovered the technical means for the fulfillment of this aspiration. In the Western world and in the Soviet Union it will take only a relatively short while until this stage is achieved, even though it will take much longer in the nonindustrialized countries of Asia, Africa, and Latin America.

Does this mean that in the rich industrial countries there is almost no longer any need for repression? This is, indeed, a widespread illusion among most people; yet it is not a fact. These societies, too, exhibit many contradictions and irrationalities. Does it make sense to spend millions of dollars on storing agricultural surpluses while

millions of people in the world are starving? Does it make
sense to spend half of the national budget on weapons
which, if and when they are used, will destroy our civilization? Does it make sense to teach children the Christian
virtues of humility and unselfishness and, at the same
time, to prepare them for a life in which the exact op-
posites of these virtues are necessary in order to be successful? Does it make sense that we fought the last two
world wars for "freedom and democracy," ending them
with the demilitarization of the "enemies of freedom," and
that only a few years later we are rearming again for
"freedom and democracy," except that the former enemies
of freedom are now its defenders, and the former allies are
the enemies? Does it make sense to be deeply indignant
against systems which do not grant freedom of speech and
of political activity, while we call the very same systems,
and even more ruthless ones, "freedom-loving" if they
have a military alliance with us? Does it make sense that
we live in the midst of plenty, yet have little joy? Does it
make sense that we are all literate, have radio and television, yet are chronically bored? Does it make sense that
. . . We could go on for many more pages, describing
the irrationalities, fictions, and contradictions of our Western way of life. Yet all these irrationalities are taken for
granted and are hardly noticed by anybody. This is by no
means due to the lack of critical capacity; we see these
same irrationalities and contradictions quite clearly in our
opponents—we only refuse to apply rational and critical
judgment to ourselves.

The repression of the awareness of facts is, and must
be, supplemented by the acceptance of many fictions. The
gaps which exist because we refuse to see many things
around us must be filled so that we may have a coherent
picture. What are these ideologies which are fed into us?
Since there are so many I will mention only a few of

them: We are Christians; we are individualists; our leaders are wise; we are good; our enemies (whoever these happen to be at the moment) are bad; our parents love us and we love them; our marriage system is successful; and so on, and so on. The Soviet states have constructed another set of ideologies: That they are Marxists; that their system is socialism; that it expresses the will of the people; that their leaders are wise and work for humanity; that the profit interest in their society is a "socialist" profit interest and different from the "capitalist" profit interest; that their respect for property is that for "socialist" property and quite different from the respect for "capitalist" property; and so on, and so on. All these ideologies are impressed on the people from childhood on by their parents, by the schools, churches, movies, television, newspapers, and they take hold of men's minds as if they were the result of the men's own thinking or observation. If this process takes place in societies opposed to ours, we call it "brain washing," and, in its less extreme forms, "indoctrination" or "propaganda"; in ours, we call it "education" and "information." Even though it is true that societies differ in the degree of awareness and brain washing, and even though the Western world is somewhat better in this respect than the Soviet world, the difference is not enough to alter the fundamental picture of a mixture between repression of facts and acceptance of fiction.[1]

Why do people repress the awareness of what they would otherwise be aware of? Undoubtedly the main reason is fear. But fear of what? Is it fear of castration, as Freud assumed? There does not seem to be sufficient evidence to believe this. Is it fear of being killed, imprisoned, or fear of starvation? That might sound like a

[1] William J. Lederer, in *A Nation of Sheep* (New York: W. W. Norton & Company, Inc., 1961), gives some good examples of this state of affairs with regard to political thinking.

satisfactory answer, provided repression occurred only in systems of terror and oppression. But since this is not so, we have to inquire further. Are there more subtle fears which a society such as our own, for instance, produces? Let us think of a young executive or engineer in a big corporation. If he has thoughts which are not "sound," he might be inclined to repress them lest he might not get the kind of promotion others get. This, in itself, would be no tragedy, were it not for the fact that he, his wife, and his friends will consider him a "failure" if he falls behind in the competitive race. Thus the fear of being a failure can become a sufficient cause for repression.

But there is still another and, as I believe, the most powerful motive for repression: the *fear of isolation and ostracism*.

For man, inasmuch as he is *man*—that is to say, inasmuch as he transcends nature and is aware of himself and of death—the sense of complete aloneness and separateness is close to insanity. Man as man is afraid of insanity, just as man as animal is afraid of death. Man has to be related, he has to find union with others, in order to be sane. This need to be one with others is his strongest passion, stronger than sex and often even stronger than his wish to live. It is this fear of isolation and ostracism, rather than the "castration fear," that makes people repress the awareness of that which is taboo since such awareness would mean being different, separate, and hence, to be ostracized. For this reason the individual must blind himself from seeing that which his group claims does not exist, or accept as truth that which the majority says is true, even if his own eyes could convince him that it is false. The herd is so vitally important for the individual that their views, beliefs, feelings, constitute reality for him, more so than what his senses and his

reason tell him. Just as in the hypnotic state of dissocia-
tion the hypnotist's voice and words take the place of
reality, so the social pattern constitutes reality for most
people. What man considers true, real, sane, are the
clichés accepted by his society, and much that does not fit
in with these clichés is excluded from awareness, is unconscious. There is almost nothing a man will not believe—or
repress—when he is threatened with the explicit or implicit
threat of ostracism. Returning to the fear of losing one's
identity which I discussed earlier, I want to state that for the
majority of people, their identity is precisely rooted in
their conformity with the social clichés. "They" are who
they are supposed to be—hence the fear of ostracism implies the fear of the loss of identity, and the very com-
bination of both fears has a most powerful effect.

The concept of ostracism as the basis of repression
could lead to the rather hopeless view that every society
can dehumanize and deform man in whatever way it likes
because every society can always threaten him with ostracism. But to assume this would mean to forget another
fact. Man is not only a member of society, but he is also
a member of the human race. While man is afraid of complete isolation from his social group, he is also afraid of
being isolated from the humanity which is inside him and
which is represented by his conscience and his reason.
To be completely inhuman is frightening, even when a
whole society has adopted inhuman norms of behavior.
The more human a society is, the less need is there for
the individual to choose between isolation from society or
from humanity. The greater the conflict between the social
aims and human aims, the more is the individual torn
between the two dangerous poles of isolation. To that
degree to which a person—because of his own intellectual
and spiritual development—feels his solidarity with humanity, can he tolerate social ostracism, and vice versa.

The ability to act according to one's conscience depends on the degree to which one has transcended the limits of one's society and has become a citizen of the world.

The average individual does not permit himself to be aware of thoughts or feelings which are incompatible with the patterns of his culture, and hence he is forced to repress them. *Formally* speaking, then, what is unconscious and what is conscious depends on the structure of society and on the patterns of feeling and thought it produces. As to the *contents of the unconscious,* no generalization is possible. But one statement can be made: it always represents the whole man, with all his potentialities for darkness and light; it always contains the basis for the different answers which man is capable of giving to the question which existence poses. In the extreme case of the most regressive cultures, bent on returning to animal existence, this very wish is predominant and conscious, while all strivings to emerge from this level are repressed. In a culture which has moved from the regressive to the spiritual-progressive goal, the forces representing the dark are unconscious. But man, in any culture, has all the potentialities within himself; he is the archaic man, the beast of prey, the cannibal, the idolater, and he is the being with a capacity for reason, for love, for justice. The content of the unconscious, then, is neither the good nor the evil, the rational nor the irrational; it is both; it is all that is human. *The unconscious is the whole man —minus that part of him which corresponds to his society.* Consciousness represents social man, the accidental limitations set by the historical situation into which an individual is thrown. Unconsciousness represents universal man, the whole man, rooted in the cosmos; it represents the plant in him, the animal in him, the spirit in him; it represents his past, down to the dawn of human existence, and it represents his future up to the day when man will have become fully human, and when nature will be humanized as man will be "naturalized." To become aware of one's unconscious means to get in touch with one's full humanity and to do away with barriers which society erects within each man and, consequently, between each man and his fellow man. To attain this aim fully is difficult and a rare occurrence; to approximate it is in the grasp of everybody, as it constitutes the emancipation of man from the socially conditioned alienation from himself and humankind. Nationalism and xenophobia are the opposite poles to the humanistic experience brought about by becoming aware of one's unconscious.

Which factors make for greater or lesser awareness of the social unconscious? First of all, it is quite obvious that certain individual experiences make a difference. The son of an authoritarian father, who has been rebelling against fatherly authority without being crushed by it, will be better prepared to see through the social rationalizations and to become aware of the social reality which, to most, is unconscious. Similarly, members of racial, religious, or social minority groups which have been discriminated against by the majority, will often be more likely to disbelieve in the social clichés; this holds also true for the members of an exploited and suffering class. But such class situation by no means always makes the individual more critical and independent. Very often his social status makes him more insecure and more eager to accept the clichés of the majority in order to be acceptable and to feel secure. It would take a minute analysis of many personal and social factors to determine why some members of minorities or exploited majorities react with increased criticism, and others with increased submission to the ruling patterns of thought.

In addition to these factors, there are purely social ones which determine how strong is the resistance against the awareness of the social reality. If a society or a social class has no chance to make any use of its insight because there is objectively no hope for a change for the better, the chances are that everybody in such a society would stick to the fictions since the awareness of the truth would only make them feel worse. Decaying societies and classes are usually those which hold most fiercely to their fictions since they have nothing to gain by the truth. Conversely, societies—or social classes—which are bound for a better future offer conditions which make the awareness of reality easier, especially if this very awareness will help them to make the necessary chances. A good example is the bourgeois class in the eighteenth century. Even before it had won political hegemony over the aristocratic class, it had shed many fictions of the past and had developed new insight into the past and present social realities. The writers of the middle classes could penetrate through the fictions of feudalism because they did not need these fictions— on the contrary, they were helped by the truth. When the bourgeois class had been firmly entrenched and was fighting against the onslaught of the working class and, later, the colonial peoples, the situation was reversed; the members of the middle classes refused to see the social reality, the members of the forward-moving new classes were more prone to dispense with many illusions. Very often, however, individuals developing these insights in support of the groups fighting for their freedom came from the very classes against which they were fighting. In all such cases one would have to examine the individual factors which make a person critical of his own social group, and make him side with the group to which he does not belong by birth.

The social and the individual unconscious are related to each other and in constant interaction. In fact, unconsciousness/consciousness is, in the last analysis, indivisible. What matters is not so much the *content* of what is repressed, but the *state of mind* and, to be more precise, the degree of awakedness and realism in the individual. If a person in a given society is not able to see the social reality, and instead fills his mind with fictions, his capacity to see the individual reality with regard to himself, his family, his friends, is also limited. He lives in a state of half-awakedness, ready to receive suggestions from all sides, and to believe that the fictions suggested to him are the truth. (Of course, a person will be particularly prone to repress the awareness of reality with regard to his personal life in areas where social repression is particularly marked. In a society, for instance, which cultivates obedience to authority, and hence repression of the awareness or criticism, the individual son will be more prone to be in awe of his father than the one in a society where criticism of authority is not an essential part of social repression.)

Freud was mainly concerned with the uncovering of the individual unconscious. While he assumed that society enforced repressions, these were the repressions of instinctual forces, and not the social repressions which really matter—the repressions of the awareness of social contradictions, socially produced suffering, of the failure of authority, of feelings of *malaise* and dissatisfaction, etc. Freudian analysis has shown that it is possible to some degree to make the individual unconscious conscious, without touching the social unconscious. However, it follows from the premises which were presented thus far, that any attempt for de-repression which excludes the social sphere must remain limited. The full awareness of what had been repressed is possible only if it transcends the individual realm, and if the process includes the analysis of the social unconscious. The reasons for this proposition follow from what has been said before. Unless a person is able to transcend his society and see how it furthers or hinders the development of human potentialities, he cannot be fully in touch with his own humanity. Socially conditioned taboos and restrictions must appear as "natural" to him, and human nature must appear in a distorted form, as long as he does not recognize the distortion of human nature by the society he happens to live in. If uncovering the unconscious means arriving at the experience of one's own humanity, then, indeed, it cannot stop with the individual but must proceed to the uncovering of the social unconscious. This implies the understanding of social dynamics and the critical appraisal of one's own society from the standpoint of universal human values. The very insight into society which Marx has given us is a condition for becoming aware of the social unconscious, and hence for the full awakening ("de-repression") of an individual. If there "should be Ego where there was Id," humanistic social criticism is a necessary precondition. Otherwise, the person will become aware only of certain aspects of his individual unconscious, yet in other aspects hardly more awake as a total person than the rest. It must be added, however, that not only is critical understanding of society important for the analytic understanding of oneself, but that the analytic understanding of the individual unconscious is also a significant contribution to the understanding of society. Only if one has experienced the dimensions of the unconscious in one's personal life can one fully appreciate how it is possible that social life is determined by ideologies which are neither truths nor lies or, to put it differently, which are both truths *and* lies—truths in the sense that people believe them sincerely, and lies in the sense that they are rationalizations which have the function of hiding the real motivation of social and political actions.

Much as the individual and the social unconscious interact, if we compare Freud's and Marx's respective concepts of repression in terms of social evolution, we find a fundamental contradiction. For Freud, as we have indicated before, growing civilization means growing repression—hence social evolution does not lead to the dissolution of repression but rather to its reinforcement. For Marx, on the other hand, repression is essentially the result of contradictions between the need for the full development of man and the given social structure—hence the fully developed society in which exploitation and class conflict have disappeared does not need ideologies and can dispense with repression. In the fully humanized society there would be no need for repression, hence there would be no social unconscious. According to Freud, repression increases; according to Marx, it decreases in the process of social evolution.

There is another difference between Freudian and Marxian thought which has not been sufficiently emphasized. While I have already discussed the similarity between "rationalization" and "ideologies," it is necessary to point to this difference. Through rationalization one tries to make it appear as though an action is motivated by reasonable and moral motives, thus covering up the fact that it is caused by motives which are in contrast to a person's conscious thinking. The rationalization is mostly sham, and has only the negative function of permitting a person to act wrongly, yet without awareness that he is acting irrationally or immorally. The ideology has a similar function, yet in one point there is an important difference. Take the example of Christian teaching: the teachings of Christ, the ideals of humility, brotherly love, justice, charity, etc., were once genuine ideals which moved the hearts of people to such a degree that they were willing to give their lives for the sake of these ideals. But throughout history these ideals have been misused to serve as rationalizations for purposes which were their very opposite. Independent and rebellious spirits have been killed, peasants have been exploited and oppressed, wars have been blessed, hatred of the enemy has been encouraged in the name of these very ideals. Inasmuch as this was the case, ideology was not different from rationalization. But history shows us that an ideology has also a life of its own. Even though the words of Christ were misused, they were kept alive, they remained in the memory of the people, and again and again they were taken seriously and retransformed, as it were, from ideologies into ideals. This happened in the Protestant sects before and after the Reformation; it is happening today in those Protestant and Catholic minorities which are fighting for peace and against hate in a world which professes to hold Christian ideals, yet uses them as ideologies. The same can be said about the "ideologization" of Buddhist ideas, of Hegel's philosophy, of Marxist thought. The task of critique is not to denounce the ideals, but to show their transformation into ideologies, and to challenge the ideology in the name of the betrayed ideal.

X
THE FATE OF BOTH THEORIES

IT IS the rule rather than the exception in the historical process that ideas deteriorate into ideologies; mere words take the place of the human reality; these words are administered by a bureaucracy which thus succeeds in controlling people and gaining power and influence. And usually the result is that the ideology, while still using the words of the original idea, in effect expresses the opposite meaning. This fate has happened to the great religions and to philosophical ideas; it has happened to Marx's and to Freud's ideas.

What was Freud's original system?

First of all it was *radical* thought; radical, in the original sense of the word, meaning going to the roots and—as Marx said—since the root is man, going to the very nature and essence of man. Freud's psychoanalysis was *critical* thought; critical first of all, of existing psychiatric ideas which took consciousness as the basic datum of psychiatry. But Freud's thought was critical in a much broader sense. It attacked many of the values and ideologies of the Victorian age; it attacked the notion that sex was not a subject for rational and scientific investigation; it attacked the insincerity of Victorian morality; it attacked the sentimental notion of the "purity" and "innocence"

135

of the child. But, as has been pointed out before, its most important attack was directed against the notion that there is no psychic content transcending consciousness. Freud's system was a challenge to existing ideas and prejudices; it opened up a new era of thought corresponding to the new development in the natural sciences and in art. It might be called in this sense a revolutionary movement, even though in spite of his criticism of some aspects of society Freud did not transcend the existing social order, nor did he think of new social and political possibilities.

What became of this radical and critical movement after the first thirty years of its existence?

First of all, psychoanalysis has become very successful, especially in the Protestant countries of Europe and in the United States, while, until the end of the First World War, it was mocked and derided by most "serious" psychiatrists and by the public in general. There were many reasons for the growing success of psychoanalysis, which will be discussed presently. The fact is that the movement, ridiculed during the first twenty years of its existence, came to be considered respectable in psychiatry, accepted by many social scientists, and popular among many literary men, some of whom—Thomas Mann, for example— were quite outstanding. But this academic and intellectual recognition was not all; psychoanalysis became popular with the public; psychoanalysts found it difficult to take all the patients who asked for their help; in fact, the profession of psychoananlysis became one of the most rewarding from the economic standpoint and from that of prestige.

This successful development, however, was by no means paralleled by a corresponding richness and productivity of psychoanalytic discoveries as regards theory and therapy. In fact, it may be surmised that the very success of psychoanalysis contributed to its deterioration. Psychoanalysis, as a whole, lost its original radicalism and its critical and challenging character. Around the beginning of the century, Freud's theories—even though they may not all have been correct—challenged existing mores and thoughts; they necessarily attracted people with a critical mind and were part of the critical movement which existed in other spheres of intellectual, political, and artistic life in Western society. But by 1930 the social mores had changed (to some extent under the influence of psychoanalysis, but mainly through the development of a consumer society which encourages consumption in all spheres and discourages the frustration of desires). Sex was no longer taboo; and to speak freely of incestuous wishes, of sexual perversions, and so on, ceased to be shocking for the urban middle class. All these topics, which an average "decent" person would not even have dared think about around 1910, lost their tabooed qualities and were accepted as the latest and not particularly exciting results of "science." In several ways psychoanalysis, instead of challenging society, conformed to it, not only in the obvious sense that since Freud's *Future of an Illusion* and *Civilization and Its Discontent*, psychoanalysts, with very few exceptions, did not produce any social criticism; but on the contrary, the vast majority of psychoanalysts represented urban middle class attitudes and tended to consider as neurotic anyone who deviated from this attitude, either to the left or to the right. Very few psychoanalysts had any serious political, philosophical, or religious interests beyond those customary in the urban middle class. This very fact points to another aspect of the deterioration of psychoanalysis: instead of being a radical movement, it became a substitute for radicalism in politics and religion. Its adherents were people who, for one reason or another, were not interested in serious political or religious problems, and thus whose lives were lacking in the meaning such interests had given to former generations. Yet, since man has a need for some philosophy which gives meaning to his life, psychoanalysis was very handy for this class. It presumed to give an all-embracing philosophy of life (even though Freud had denied such an intention explicitly). Many a psychoanalyzed person believed that he had solved all the riddles of life by means of the concepts of the Oedipus complex, the fear of castration, etc.; that if the whole world could be psychoanalyzed, or at least all its leaders, there would be no serious political problems left for man to solve.

The modern individual, even more isolated and lonely than his grandfather was, finds a solution in psychoanalysis. First of all he is a member of a somewhat esoteric cult; he is one of the "initiated" who has gone through the ritual of analysis, now knows all the secrets worth knowing, and thus is part of a cult. Furthermore, he has the satisfaction of having found somebody who listens sympathetically and without accusing him. This factor is particularly important in a society where hardly anybody listens to anybody. While people *talk* to each other, they do not *listen* to each other, except for a superficial and polite "hearing" of what the other says. In addition, the psychoanalyst's significance has been inflated by the person being analyzed ("transference"); the analyst is converted into a hero whose assistance in living is as important as that of the priest was in a religious world, or the big or small *Fuehrer* in certain political systems. Beyond that, psychoanalysis, with its emphasis on early childhood experiences as being the cause for later development, tended to relieve many persons of a sense of responsibility. They believed that all one had to do was to talk and talk until one had recalled the childhood traumas—after which happiness would follow as a matter of course. Many people believed in this achievement of "happiness by talking" and forgot that nothing in life is achieved without effort, daring to take risks and often some suffering. Paying the analyst, talking for five hours a week on the couch, and some anxiety produced when the resistance grows, were often considered as the equivalent of effort and daring. But, if at all, they are a rather insufficient equivalent. This holds especially true for the upper middle class, for which neither the money nor the time represent any serious sacrifice.

What does the patient want? If he has serious symptoms such as psychogenetic headaches, or a wash compulsion, or if he suffers from sexual impotence, he wants to be cured of his symptoms. This is what motivated most of Freud's patients to seek analytic help. In general it is not too difficult to cure such symptoms psychoanalytically and it is, if anything, an underestimation to assume that at least 50 percent of such patients are cured. But in the last twenty years these patients with symptoms no longer constitute the majority of those seeking the help of the psychoanalyst. An increasing number of people come who do not suffer from any "symptom" in the traditional sense, but who suffer from what the French called over a century ago *la maladie du siécle;* they suffer from a general unhappiness, from lack of satisfaction in their work, from lack of happiness in their marriages, from the fact that "they are without joy in the midst of plenty," to use a Biblical expression. This new type of patient often seeks nothing but the relief which the psychoanalytic procedure can give, even when it is not successful; the satisfaction of having somebody to talk to, of "belonging" to a cult, of having a "philosophy." The aim of therapy is often that of helping the person to be better adjusted to existing circumstances, to "reality" as it is frequently called; mental health is often considered to be nothing but this adjustment or, to put it differently, a state of mind in which one's individual unhappiness is reduced to the level of the general unhappiness. The *real* problem, that of man's loneliness and alienation, of his lack of a productive interest in life, need not even be touched in this type of psychoanalysis.

One cannot talk about the aim of "adjustment" which much of contemporary psychoanalysis has without mentioning at least the problem of the function of psychology in contemporary industrial society. This is a society which needs to make man fit in a complicated and hierarchically organized system of production with a minimum of friction. It creates the organization man, a man without conscience or conviction, but one who is proud of being a cog, even if it is only a small one, in a big and imposing organization. He is not to ask questions, not to think critically, not to have any passionate interests, for this would impede the smooth functioning of the organization. But man is not made to be a thing, he is not made to shun asking questions. Hence, in spite of "job security," "old-age pensions," and the satisfaction of belonging to a large and "nationally known" outfit, man is disquieted and not happy. Here the psychologist comes in. By his tests he has already eliminated the more adventurous and rebellious types, and for those who are still not happy with the organization life he offers relief by letting them "express" themselves, by giving them the satisfaction that somebody listens to them and, eventually—and most importantly—by making it clear to them that lack of adjustment is a kind of neurosis, thus helping them to remove those tendencies which stand in the way of full adjustment. The psychologists, using the "right" words from Socrates to Freud, become the priests of industrial society, helping to fulfill its aims by helping the individual to become the perfectly adjusted organization man.

To return from the role of psychology in an industrial society to the specific problem of psychoanalysis and its deterioration, one more factor must be mentioned: that of the bureaucratization of the psychoanalytic movement itself. It is true that Freud was somewhat authoritarian in his attitude toward the purity of his own system. Yet it must be considered that he had developed a most original system against which a tremendous resistance arose from all sides. It might have been easy to protect it from his overt enemies, but it was much more difficult to protect it from those adherents who, while consciously being in agreement with Freud, succumbed to the temptation of making it more palatable to society, and hence to falsify it. Freud, concerned with preserving the purity and the radicalism of his teaching, appointed a secret council of seven, to watch over the development of psychoanalysis. But this council soon developed the typical features which characterize a ruling bureaucracy. There were violent jealousies among its members. Those between Jones on the one hand, and Ferenczi and Rank on the other, are well known. These rivalries found a drastic expression in the fact that Jones, after both were dead, wrote in his biography of Freud that both rivals had suffered from insanity before their deaths, a statement which is contrary to the facts.[1]

The more the movement grew, the more did the leading bureaucracy, by now consisting of many new members, try to control it. This was no longer a defense against those who, because of lack of courage, tried to tune down Freud's teachings. On the contrary, as has been said before, official psychoanalysis had lost its radical character, and very often the aim of the bureaucracy was to remove and keep out the more radical analysts. Control of the ideology meant control of the movement and its members, and was so used. Old members who did not entirely agree with the dogma were excluded or forced to resign, others were crit-

---

[1] Cf. a detailed discussion of this point in E. Fromm, *Sigmund Freud's Mission,* World Perspective Series, edited by Ruth Nanda Anshen (New York: Harper & Brothers, 1959).

icized by the London authorities even for having shown a
"bored face" while listening to a speech by an orthodox
representative of the bureaucracy. Psychoanalysts (in fact,
though not in form) were forbidden—as recently as 1961
—to give lectures at scientific meetings of groups of analysts who were not members of the official organization. It
is not surprising that the bureaucratization of the psychoanalytic movement resulted in a corresponding diminution
of scientific creativity. Many new ideas in psychoanalysis were expressed by analysts who sooner or later
severed their ties with the bureaucracy and continued their
work outside of its jurisdiction.

What has become of Marxist thought in the more than
hundred years of its existence? Here again we must begin
with a statement of what it was originally, and that means
essentially in the time from the middle of the nineteenth
century to the beginning of the World War of 1914. The
Marxist theory, as well as the socialist movement, was radical and humanistic—radical in the above-mentioned sense
of going to the roots, and the roots being man; humanistic
in the sense that it is man who is the measure of all things,
that his full unfolding must be the aim and the criterion
of all social efforts. The liberation of man from the strangle
hold of economic conditions which prevented his full development was the aim of all of Marx's thought and efforts. Socialism in these first fifty or sixty years was,
though not in theological language, the most important authentic spiritual movement in the Western world.

What became of it? It became successful, gained power,
and in this very process succumbed to its opponent—the
spirit of capitalism. This development is not too surprising.
Capitalism was successful beyond anything the early socialists could have visualized. Instead of leading to an ever increasing misery of the workers, the progress of technology
and of the organization of capitalist society made it pos-

sible for the workers to benefit from its advances. True enough, this happened to some extent at the expense of colonial peoples; and furthermore, it happened to some extent through the fight of the socialist parties and trade unions for a greater share in the social product. But whatever the role of these various factors may have been, the result is that the workers and their leaders were more and more captivated by the spirit of capitalism and began to interpret socialism in accordance with capitalist principles. While Marxism had aimed at a humanist society transcending capitalism, a society which would have as its aim the full unfolding of the individual personality, the majority of socialists regarded socialism as a movement to improve the economic and socio-political situation *within* capitalism; they considered the socialization of the means of production, plus the principles of the welfare state as a sufficient criterion of a socialist society. The principles of this type of "socialism" were essentially the same as those of capitalism: maximum economic efficiency, large-scale bureaucratically organized industry, and subordination of the individual under this bureaucratic but economically efficient system.

Basically the majority of socialists in the West and in the East shared this capitalistic interpretation of socialism, but, according to their respective economic and political positions, they arrived at different solutions. The Western leaders began to make their peace with capitalism at the beginning of the war of 1914. Instead of remaining faithful to their basic doctrine of peace and internationalism, the socialist leaders of both camps supported their governments, claiming that they were supporting the war for the sake of freedom, because they had the good luck to be fighting the Kaiser and the Czar, respectively. When the imperial system in Germany collapsed as the result of prolonging a virtually lost war far beyond any reasonable consideration, the same leaders formed a secret alliance with the generals in order to defeat the revolution. They permitted first the growth of the Reichswehr, and of secret and half-secret semimilitary organizations which became the basis of Nazi power—and they virtually capitulated completely before the increasing strength and oppressiveness of the Nazi and nationalistic right wing forces. The French socialist leaders followed a similar direction, which led the French socialist party under the leadership of Guy Mollet to the open support of the Algerian war. In England, as in the Scandinavian countries, the situation was somewhat different. In these countries the socialists won majorities, either temporarily or more or less continuously, and used their strength to build a welfare state. A highly developed system of social security and particularly of a social health service, brought to its full fruition the system which had been started by conservatives in Europe in the nineteenth century (Disraeli in England and Bismarck in Germany), and which was started in the United States under the leadership of F. D. Roosevelt in the thirties. In addition, the British Labour Party socialized some of the key industries, believing that such socialization of the means of production was the touchstone of true socialism. But while they satisfied the economic interests of the workers, their brand of socialism ceased to be the vision of a fundamental change of the human condition. They lost one election after another and sought to recoup their losses by giving up almost all radical aims. The same process occurred in Germany, where the Social Democratic Party not only gave up almost all socialist aims, but also accepted the principles of nationalism and rearmament to such an extent that the social democratic policy is hardly distinguishable from that of their opponents.

What happened in Russia was apparently the opposite of the Western development, and yet there are certain similarities. Russia, in contrast to the Western European countries, had not yet become a fully industrialized country in spite of the fact that the industry that existed was highly developed; three-quarters of the population were peasants, most of them poor. The Czarist administration was corrupt and largely incompetent and, in addition to all this, the war of 1914 had bled the Russian people without bringing them victory. The first revolution of 1917, led by Kerenski and others, failed mainly because of the unwillingness of the leaders to end the war, and thus Lenin was confronted with the task of taking over power in a country which did not have the economic conditions which, according to Marx's thinking, were necessary for the building of a socialist system. Logically, Lenin put all his hopes in the outbreak of a socialist revolution in Western Europe, and especially in Germany. But these hopes failed to materialize, and the Bolshevik revolution was confronted with an insoluble task. By 1922–23 it was perfectly clear that the hope for a German revolution had completely lost its basis at the same time Lenin became gravely ill and died in 1924. He was spared having to solve the final dilemma.

Stalin, using the names of Marx and Lenin, in reality devoted himself to building up a state-capitalism in Russia. He organized an industrial monopoly of the state led by a new managerial bureaucracy, and employed a method of centralized, bureaucratic industrialization which was also developing in Western capitalism, although less completely and drastically. In order to transform a peasant population into one with the work discipline necessary for modern industrialism, and, furthermore, in order to induce the population to accept the sacrifices in consumption necessary for the rapid accumulation of capital to be used for the construction of basic industries, he used two means: one, force and terror, although—due to his own mad suspiciousness and his unlimited desire for personal power—a terror which went far beyond what would have been necessary for the above-mentioned economic aims, and which, in fact, in many ways weakened his economic and military position. The other means Stalin used was the same as in capitalism: the incentive of increased income for better and more work. This incentive is the most important one used to improve the efficiency of workers, managers, and peasants. In fact, any capitalistic manager convinced that the "profit motive" is the only efficient motivation for progress would be delighted with the Russian system, especially if he is opposed to the interference of trade unions in the managerial function.[1]

In the years until Stalin's death, the Soviet Union had built a sufficient basis for increased consumption; it had also trained its population sufficiently in industrial work discipline to permit the end of terror and the construction of a police state. While this state does not permit the expression of opinions critical of the system, and even less of corresponding political activity, it has freed the average citizen from the fright of being arrested in the early-morning hours for expressing critical thoughts, or simply because of the denunciation by a personal enemy.

The degradation of Stalin, finding its completion at the Congress of the Communist Party in the fall of 1961, and the new program of the Communist Party accepted by the same Congress, are the final steps marking the transition from the Stalinist phase to the Khrushchevist phase in the Soviet Union. This phase can be characterized as consisting of various elements: economically, a completely centralized state capitalism, bringing the monopolistic principle of contemporary industrialism to its final develop-

---

[1] Cf. for a more detailed analysis of these points E. Fromm, *May Man Prevail?: An Inquiry into the Facts and Fictions of Foreign Policy* (New York: Doubleday & Company, Inc., and Anchor Books, 1961), pp. 46–86.

ment; socially, a welfare state which takes care of the basic social and economic needs of the whole population; politically, a police state which restricts freedom of opinion and political activity, yet which has a considerable amount of legalism, protecting the citizens from arbitrary police measures. The citizen knows what he can do and what he cannot do and, provided he moves within these limits, he need not be afraid. Culturally and psychologically the Khrushchevist system proclaims a Calvinistic work ethic, and a strict morality centered around fatherland, work, family, and duty—a morality more similar to the ideas of Pétain or Salazar than to those of Marx. The Soviet Union today is a conservative "have" state, more reactionary in many ways than the "capitalist" states, more progressive in one essential point—namely, that private corporate interests cannot interfere with the general political and economic plans of the government.

The Soviet system still uses revolutionary and socialist ideas voiced by Marx, Engels, and Lenin as ideologies which give a sense of meaning to the masses. Yet they have lost effectiveness, and the situation can be compared with that of the West, where the Christian idea is still used but mainly ideologically, that is, without an effective basis in the hearts and actions of most of the people who profess these ideas.

The foregoing description of the history of the psychoanalytic and the socialist movements ends on the tragic note of stating their failure. However, while this statement is correct as far as the established great bureaucracies are concerned, it does not take into account more hopeful aspects.

Psychoanalytic radicalism has not been killed by the bureaucracy, and psychoanalytic thought has not been stifled either. A number of psychoanalysts, much as they differ among themselves, have tried to find new ways and to create new concepts. They all have their fountainhead in Freud's classic discoveries of the unconscious processes, but they have made use of new therapeutic experiences, of progress in biology and medicine, of new ways of thinking spurred on by philosophy and theoretical physics. In fact, some of them take a position very close to Freud's; the main elements common to all these various trends lie in the fact that they have liberated themselves from the thought control of the psychoanalytic bureaucracy, and have made full use of this freedom in developing creatively psychoanalytic theory and therapy.

Socialism, being a movement of incomparably greater historic significance than psychoanalysis, has also not been destroyed by its enemies, nor by its "representatives," right or left. All over the world there are small groups of radical humanist socialists who express and revise Marxist socialism, and who try to contribute to the growth of a humanist socialism which is as different from Soviet communism as it is from capitalism. These voices which express the spirit of Marx are still weak and isolated; yet they exist, and they give rise to the hope that if mankind will avoid the supreme madness of nuclear war, a new international socialist movement will realize the principles and promises of Western and Eastern Humanism.

XI

SOME RELATED IDEAS

THERE are still ideas left which are premises—or consequences—of the concepts discussed in the
bulk of this book, yet which did not fall precisely under
any one of the chapter headings dealing with Freud's and
Marx's concepts. In this present chapter I shall try to
deal with some of these related ideas.

The first of these ideas deals with the connection between "thought" and "concern." Both psychology and sociology have as their object *man*. I can get to know a great
deal *about* man by observing him like any other object. I
—the observer—stand against my "ob-ject" ("ob-ject" and
"objection" have the same root; in German, *Gegenstand*
= "counterstand") to observe it, describe it, measure it,
weigh it—yet I do not *understand* that which is alive
if it remains an "object." I understand man only in the
situation of being related to him, when he ceases to be a
split-off object and becomes part of me or, to be still more
correct, when he becomes "me," yet remains also "not-me."
If I remain a distant observer I see only manifest behavior,
and if this is all I want to know, I can be satisfied with
being an observer. But in this position the whole of the
other person, his full reality, escapes me. I have described
him from this and the other aspect—yet I have never met

him. Only if I am open to him and respond to him, and that is, precisely, if I am related to him, do I see my fellow man; and to see him is to know him.

How can I see the other if I am filled with myself? To be filled with oneself means to be filled with one's own image, with one's greed, or with one's anxiety. But it does not mean "being oneself." Indeed, I need to be myself in order to see the other. How could I understand his fear, his sadness, his aloneness, his hope, his love—unless I felt my own fear, sadness, aloneness, hope, or love? If I cannot mobilize my own human experience, mobilize it and engage myself with my fellow man, I might come to know a great deal *about* him, but I shall never know *him*. To be open is the condition to enable me to become filled with him, to become soaked with him, as it were; but *I* need to be *I,* otherwise how could *I* be open? I need to be myself, that is, my own authentic, unique self, in order to throw out myself, in order to transcend the illusion of the reality of this unique self. As long as I have not established my own identity, as long as I have not fully emerged from the womb, from the family, from the ties of race and nation— in other words, as long as I have not fully become an individual, a free man, I cannot throw away this individual and thus experience that I am nothing but the drop of water on the crest of the wave, a separate entity for a split of a second.

Being related, being engaged, means to be concerned. If I am a participant rather than a distant observer, I become interested (*inter-esse* means "to-be-in"). "To-be-in" means not to be outside. If "I-am-in," then the world becomes my concern. This concern *can* be one of destruction. The "interest" of the suicidal person in himself is the interest to destroy himself, just as the "interest" of the homicidal person in the world is that of destroying it. But this latter interest is a pathological one; not because "man is good," but because it is the very quality of life that it tends to sustain itself; *"to-be-in"* the world means to be concerned with the life and the growth of myself and all other beings.

Concerned knowledge, the "being-in" knowledge, then, leads to the desire to help; it is, if we use the word in a broad sense, therapeutically oriented knowledge. This quality of concerned knowledge has found its classic expression in Buddhist thought. When the Buddha saw an old man, a sick man, a dead man, he did not remain a distant observer; he was moved to think about the question how man can be saved from suffering. It was his concern to help man which led the Buddha to his discovery that if man can liberate himself from his greed and ignorance, he can liberate himself from suffering. Once the orientation to the world has become one of passionate concern, all thinking about the world takes different paths. The simplest example for this is offered by medicine. How many medical discoveries would have been made without the wish to heal? It is the same concern which underlies all Freud's discoveries. Had he not been prompted by the wish to cure mental disturbances, how could he have discovered the unconscious in the various disguises in which it appears in symptoms and dreams? Quite obviously, random and uninterested observation rarely leads to significant knowledge. All questions posed by the intellect are determined by our interest. This interest, far from being opposed to knowledge, is its very condition, provided it is blended with reason, that is, with the capacity to see things as they are, "to let them be."

I was greatly helped in seeing this by my activity as a psychoanalyst. I had been trained in accordance with the strictly orthodox Freudian procedure of analyzing a patient while sitting behind him and listening to his associations. This technique of psychoanalysis was modeled along the lines of the laboratory experiment: the patient was the "object," the analyst observed his free associations, dreams, etc., and analyzed the material produced by the patient. The analyst was supposed to be a distant observer, a mirror, rather than a participant. The longer I worked in this manner, the less did I feel satisfied. First of all, I often became tired and even sleepy during the analytic work; I often felt relieved when the analytic hour was over. But worse than that, I had less and less the feeling that I really understood the patient. To be sure, I had learned to "interpret," and I had learned enough so as to interpret in such a way that usually the patient's associations and dreams fitted into my theoretical expectations. But I still was talking *about* the patient rather than *to him*—and I felt that much of what I ought to understand was escaping me. At first I thought, quite naturally, that all these doubts were due to my lack of experience. But when the doubts grew with my experience instead of decreasing, I began to have doubts about the method I was using. Stimulated and encouraged by colleagues who had had similar experiences, I began to grope about to find a new way. Eventually I found this to be a simple one: instead of being an observer, I had to become a participant; to be engaged with the patient; from center to center, rather than from periphery to periphery. I discovered that I could begin to see things in the patient which I had not observed before, that I began to understand *him,* rather than to *interpret* what he said, and that I hardly ever felt tired any more during the analytic hour. At the same time I experienced that one could be fully objective while being fully engaged. "Objective" here means to see the patient as he is, and not as I want him to be. But to be objective is only possible if one does not want anything for oneself, neither the patient's admiration, nor his submission, nor even his "cure." If the latter sounds like a contradiction of what I said before, namely, that is precisely the wish to help which fertilizes one's thinking, I want to stress that, in fact, there is no contradiction. In the genuine wish to help I want nothing for myself, I am neither hurt in my self-esteem when the patient does not improve, nor am I elated about "my" achievement when he gets well.

What holds true for psychology holds true also for sociology. If I am not concerned with society, then my thinking about society has no focus; it is nothing more than a blind groping, even if the blindness is hidden by a collection of "data" and impressive statistics. If I am concerned with man—and how can concern with the individual man be separated from concern with the society of which he is a part?—I am struck with the suffering that society causes, and I am prompted by the wish to reduce the suffering so as to help man to become fully human. If one is concerned with man, then this concern poses various questions: how can man be free, how can he be fully human, how can he become what he could be? It was this concern which prompted Marx to make his great discoveries. They, like any other scientific discovery, were not all correct; in fact, the history of science is the history of errors. This holds true for Marx's as it does for Freud's theories. What matters is not that a new insight is necessarily the last word of truth, but that it is fruitful, that it is conducive to further discovery, and more than that: that in discovering truth, man changes himself because he becomes more awake and can transmit this greater awakedness to those who follow after him.

The interrelation between concern and knowledge has often been expressed—and rightly so—in terms of the interrelation between theory and practice. As Marx once wrote, one must not only interpret the world, but one must change it. Indeed, interpretation without intention of change is empty; change without interpretation is blind. Interpretation and change, theory and practice, are not two separate factors which can be combined; they are interrelated in such a way that knowledge becomes fertilized by practice and practice is guided by knowledge; theory and practice both change their nature once they cease to be separate.

The problem of the interrelation between theory and practice has still another facet, the connection between *intelligence* and *character*. To be sure, every individual is born with a certain level of intelligence, and no psychological factors are responsible for his being either an idiot or a genius. But idiots and geniuses are exceptions; what impressed me more and more was the stupidity of the vast majority of people who do not fall under either of these extreme categories. I am not referring to the lack of the sort of intelligence which is measured by intelligence tests, but to the incapacity for understanding the less obvious causes of phenomena, of grasping contradictions within the same phenomenon, of making connections between different and not obviously related factors. This stupidity is most apparent in the views people have about personal relationships and social affairs. Why is it that people cannot see the most obvious facts in personal and social affairs and, instead, cling to clichés which are endlessly repeated without ever being questioned? Intelligence, aside from the native faculty, is largely a function of independence, courage, and aliveness; stupidity is equally a result of submission, fear, and inner deadness. If an essential part of intelligence consists in the ability to make connections between factors which so far have not been seen as being related, the person who sticks to the cliché and to convention will not dare to recognize such connections; the person who is afraid of being different will not dare to recognize fictions for what they are, and hence will be greatly impeded from uncovering reality. The little boy in the story of the emperor's clothes who sees that the emperor is naked, is, after all, not more intelligent than the adults, but he is not yet so eager to conform. Furthermore, any new discovery is an adventure, and the adventures require not only a certain degree of inner security, but also a vitality and joy which can be found only in those for whom living is more than releasing tensions and avoiding pain. In order to reduce the general level of stupidity, we need not more "intellect" but a different kind of character: men who are independent, adventurous, and who are in love with life.

I cannot leave the topic of intellect without talking about another aspect, the danger of intellectualization and of the misuse of words. Words can be used without meaning what they purport to mean; words can be empty shells and one can learn certain philosophical, religious, and political ideas as one learns a foreign language. *Indeed one of the greatest dangers to be avoided is to confuse words with facts; the fetishism of words prevents the understanding of reality.*

This can be observed in all areas—most of all, perhaps, in religion, politics, and philosophy. The vast majority of all Americans believe in God; yet from all observations, scientifically organized as well as random observations, it seems clear that this belief in God has very little consequence for action and the conduct of life. Most people are concerned with health, money, and "education" (the latter as part of social success), and not at all with the problems which would arise if they were concerned with God. We are consumption-hungry and production-proud, and show precisely all the traits of materialism of which we accuse the "godless." If there is anything to be taken seriously in our profession of God, it is to recognize the fact that God has become an idol. Not an idol of wood or stone like the ones our ancestors worshiped, but an idol of words, phrases, doctrines. We violate at every moment the command not to use God's name in vain, which means using his name emptily, and not as the stammering expression of an inexpressible experience. We consider people to be "religious" because they say that they believe in God. Is there any difficulty in *saying* this? Is there any reality in it, except that words are uttered?

Obviously I am speaking here about an experience which should constitute the reality behind the words. What is this experience? It is one of recognizing oneself as part of humanity, of living according to a set of values in which the full experience of love, justice, truth, is the dominant goal of life to which everything else is subordinated; it means a constant striving to develop one's powers of love and reason to a point at which a new harmony with the world is attained; it means to strive for humility, to see one's identity with all beings, and to give up the illusion of a separate, indestructible ego. And it means not to confuse what belongs to Caesar with that which belongs to God. In the realm of Caesar, one man has more power than another, more talent, more intelligence, more achievement. But in the spiritual realm, no man is superior to another, nor inferior either. In this realm we are all nothing other than human—saints *and* criminals, heroes *and* cowards. To arrive at the authentic experience, where the realm of "Caesar" and the realm of "God" are no longer confused, is an essential part of the reality behind the words which say, "Give to Caesar that which is Caesar's and to God that which is God's."

This distinction between the two realms touches upon another of the most significant aspects of religious experience, the attitude towards power. The realm of Caesar is the realm of power. In our physical existence we all are subject to power. Anyone who has a pistol can kill us or imprison us; anyone who controls the means of our livelihood can starve us or force us to do his bidding. Inasmuch as we want to live, we must submit or fight—provided there is a chance—and there often is none. Precisely because power decides upon life and death, freedom and slavery, it impresses not only our bodies but our minds. The one who controls superior force is admired and sanctified. He is supposed to be all-wise and even all-good, even though he enslaves us; for we prefer to submit "voluntarily" to the "good" and "wise" ones, rather than to accept the fact that we are helpless to refuse obedience to the wicked ones. As long as we glorify power we accept the values of Caesar; and if we link God with power, then indeed, we commit the utmost sacrilege of transforming God into Caesar. Yet this is precisely what man has done for thousands of years. Genuine spiritual experience knows the *facts* of power— but it never glorifies power as the bearer of wisdom or goodness. Its motto is the prophet's words: "Not by might and not by power but by my spirit, speaks the Lord."

The evolution of religion is closely interwoven with development of man's self-awareness and individuation. It seems that with the development of self-awareness, man developed also the experience of his aloneness and separateness from others. This experience leads to intense anxiety and, in order to overcome this anxiety, man developed the passionate desire to be united with the world, to cease being separate. For hundreds of thousands of years he attempted to return to where he had come from, to become one again with nature. He wanted to be again one with the animal, one with the trees; he wanted to escape the burden of being human, of having consciousness of himself and of the world. He tried to achieve this union in many ways. He worshiped trees and rivers, he identified himself with animals and sought for fulfilment by feeling and acting like an animal. Or, he tried to eliminate his consciousness, to forget that he was human, by taking intoxicants, drugs, or by sexual orgies. Eventually he made himself idols into whom he projected all he had, to whom he sacrificed his children and his cattle, in order to feel part of the idol, and strong and powerful in this symbiosis. Yet, at one point of history, very recently indeed, less than four thousand years ago, man made a decisive turn. He recognized that he could never find unity by eliminating his humanity; that he could never return to the innocence of paradise; that he could never solve the problem of being a man, of transcending nature and yet being in it, by going backward. He recognized that he could solve his problem only by moving forward, by developing fully his reason and his love, by becoming fully human and thus finding a new harmony with man and nature, feeling again at home in the world.

This new insight was experienced in many different places in the world between 1500 B.C. and 500 B.C. Lao-tse discovered it in China, the Buddha in India, Eknaton in Egypt, Moses in Palestine, the philosophers in Greece. The experience which lay behind these different discoveries may not have been precisely the same; in fact there are not even two individuals who have precisely the same experience. But they were essentially the same; and yet they were formulated in entirely different ways. Lao-tse and the Buddha did not speak of a God at all; Lao-tse spoke of the "Way," the Buddha of Nirvana and Enlightenment. The Greek philosophers spoke of a principle, a primordial substance, or an unmoved mover. On the other hand, the Egyptians and the Hebrews used an entirely different concept; having the tradition of centralized yet small states with a powerful royal figure, they conceived of a supreme being, the ruler of heaven and earth. The Hebrews fought against idols, they prohibited making any kind of image of God; Maimonides, their greatest philosopher, a thousand years later declared that even to mention a positive attribute of God was not permissible. Yet the thought concept of God as the form under which the inexpressible was expressed, was retained in Judaism and in Christianity, and thus became the dominant concept of religious experience in the Western world. Many in the eighteenth and nineteenth centuries protested against this thought concept, together with their protest against kings and emperors. In the enlightenment philosophy and in the new humanism, the experience underlying religious tradition was expressed in nontheistic terms—in the concern for man, rather than in concern for God. Yet the concern was the same. It was a concern for man's full development, for making him an end and not a means, for creating the social conditions for the spiritual development of man. The socialism of Marx, Fourier, Kropotkin, Owen, Jaurès, Rosa Luxemburg, and Gorki was the most important genuine religious movement of the last hundred years. The breakdown of the humanistic tradition, beginning with the World War of 1914, almost completely destroyed this nontheistic "religious" movement. Nietzsche said that God was dead; what happened after 1914 was that man was dead. Only in small circles and among a few individuals did the humanist spiritual tradition continue; its greatest representatives in our times are men like Gandhi, Einstein, and Schweitzer.

The fetishism of words is as dangerous in the realm of political ideology as it is in that of religious ideology. Words have to be seen together with the deeds and with the total personality of him who utters them. Words have meaning only in the total context of deed and character; unless there is unity among these factors words serve to deceive— others and oneself; instead of revealing, they have the function of hiding. All this was driven home to many by the historical period in which we lived. Most of the socialist leaders who had spoken the language of internationalism and peace before August 2, 1914, participated in the war hysteria a day later. The same leaders four years later prevented any effective socialization after the German revolution, by using the slogan "Socialism is marching." The socialist

Mussolini became the leader of fascism; yet until the day of his betrayal, his words were not different from those of other socialists. Hitler called his system, the aim of which was to serve German heavy industry and expansionism toward East and West, "national socialism"; Stalin called his system "socialism," a system which served the rapid build-up of an industrialized Russia with complete disregard for all those human values which characterized Marxist socialism. Yet his friends as well as his enemies took the words for realities. We do the same by calling Franco and other dictators "representatives of the free world."

The fetishism of words is the opposite of the recognition of reality, and man's search for reality and his own increasing approximation of it characterizes his development. His search for reality is at the same time his negation of illusions. The Buddha, Moses, the Greek philosophers, the new science, the enlightenment philosophers, the great artists, the great physicists, biologists, chemists, Marx and Freud—they all have in common the passionate desire to break through the deceptive "Maya" of the senses and of "common sense" and to arrive at a perception of human and natural, of spiritual and material reality. Their fields differed, their methods differed, but no doubt their impulse and goal was the same. All that the human race has achieved, spiritually and materially, it owes to the destroyers of illusions and to the seekers of reality.

The search for reality and the uncovering of illusions not only produces insight and knowledge, it changes man in the process. His eyes are opened, he awakens, he sees the world as it is and, correspondingly, he learns how to use and develop his own intellectual and affective powers in order to cope with reality. Only the one whose eyes have been opened is a realist. It is not accidental that the most creative men and women in the arts and sciences today, with very few exceptions, stand on one side. They

share the conviction of the need for international understanding, for the political and economic emancipation of
the nonindustrialized nations, for the need to end war and
the armament race, for the faith that man is capable of becoming fully human, and that he must decide for life and
against death. Yet these leaders of our civilization are accused by "realists" of being "sentimental," "soft," and
"unrealistic." The spokesmen for "realism" claim, contrary
to all historical evidence, that an ever more acute arms
race can preserve peace; they play around with a balance
sheet of destruction according to which sixty million dead
Americans are "acceptable," while one hundred million
may not be "acceptable." They speak of shelter programs
which are to protect the population, and they invent fantastic arguments in order to avoid stating the fact that, in
the event of thermonuclear war, in all likelihood almost all
the inhabitants of our big cities will be destroyed within
seconds and hours, shelters or not. These "realists" do not
know that they are being most unrealistic. In the past
the various sectors of human society were so independent
of each other, that when the "realists" of one civilization
led it to destruction, other civilizations could continue
flourishing. Today the human race is so intertwined that
one group of mad "realists" can put an end to the valiant
efforts of hundreds of generations.

It is difficult to know to what extent a man born in 1900
can convey his experience to people born after 1914, or
after 1929, or after 1945. I selected these dates, of course,
intentionally. Anyone who was, like myself, at least four-
teen years of age when the First World War broke out,
still experienced part of the solid, secure world of the
nineteenth century. To be sure, if he was born as the son
of a middle-class family with all necessities and quite a
few luxuries provided, he experienced a much more comfortable aspect of this prewar period than if he had been

born into a poor family. Yet even for the majority of the population, and especially for the working class, the end of the last and the beginning of the present century were a tremendous improvement over the conditions of existence even fifty years earlier, and they were filled with hope for a better future.

It is difficult for the generations born after 1914 to appreciate to what extent this war shattered the foundations of Western civilization. This war broke out against the will of everybody, yet with the connivance of most participants or, rather, of special interest groups in each country which exercised sufficient pressure to make the war possible. By and large, Europeans, after almost one hundred years without major and catastrophic wars, and almost fifty years after the German-French war, were prone to think that "it can't happen." The powerful Socialist International seemed to be resolved to prevent war. The antiwar and pacifist movement was a potent force. But even the governments, whether that of the Czar, of the Kaiser, or of France and England, seemed to be resolved to avoid war. Yet it did happen. Reason and decency seemed suddenly to have left Europe. The same socialist leaders who only months before had pledged themselves to international solidarity, now hurled at each other the vilest nationalistic epithets. The nations that had known and admired each other, suddenly broke out in a mad paroxysm of hate. The British became cowardly mercenaries to the Germans; the Germans became vile Huns to their enemies; the music of Bach and Mozart became tainted; French words in the German language were ostracized. Not only that, but the moral rule against the killing of civilians was broken. Both sides bombed helpless cities and killed women and children; it was mainly the lack of development in aviation that restricted the scope and intensity of these raids. But the fate of the soldiers was equally in contrast to all demands of humanity. Millions on both sides were forced to attack the enemy trenches and were killed in the process, although it should have been clear that such tactics had become futile. But perhaps worst of all, the slaughter was based on a lie. The Germans were persuaded that they were fighting for freedom, and so were their Western enemies. When the chips were down, especially when, after 1916, a possibility for peace arose, both sides refused to settle because both insisted on gaining the territories for which the war was really being fought—regardless of the cost. At one point millions of men recognized the great deception. They rebelled against those who forced them to continue the slaughter, in Russia and Germany successfully, in France sporadically, by means of mutinies which were severely punished by the generals.

What had happened? The belief in continuing progress and peace had been shattered, moral principles which had seemed secure were violated. The unthinkable had happened. Yet hope had not disappeared. After the first step in brutalization, hope arose again in the minds of men. It is important to understand this because nothing is more characteristic of Western history than the principle of hope which had governed it for two thousand years.

As I said before, the First World War shattered this hope but did not yet destroy it. Men rallied their energies and tried to take up the task where it had been interrupted in 1914. Many believed that the League of Nations would bring about the beginning of a new era of peace and reason; others, that the Russian revolution would overcome its Czarist heritage and would develop into a true humanist-socialist society; aside from this, people in the capitalist countries believed that their system would follow a straight line of economic progress. The years between 1929 and 1933 shattered what was left of these hopes.

The capitalist system showed that it was not capable of preventing unemployment and misery for a large part of the population. In Germany the people permitted Hitler to come to power and thus began a regime of archaic irrationality and ruthless cruelty. In Russia, after Stalin had transformed the revolution into a conservative state capitalism, he initiated a system of terror which was as ruthless, or more so, than that of the Nazis. While all this was happening, the approaching World War was already becoming visible on the horizon. The brutalization which had begun in 1914, which had been followed by the systems of Stalin and Hitler, now came to its full fruition. The Germans initiated it by their air attacks on Warsaw, Amsterdam, and Coventry. The Western allies followed by their attacks on Cologne, Hamburg, Leipzig, Tokyo and, finally, with the dropping of the atomic bomb on Hiroshima and Nagasaki. In hours or minutes, hundred thousands of men, women, and children were killed in one city, and all this with few scruples and hardly any remorse. Indiscriminate destruction of human life had become a legitimate means for attaining political goals. The process of increasing brutalization had done its work. Each side brutalizes the other, following the logic "if he is inhuman I must (and can) be inhuman too."

The war ended, and there arose a new flicker of hope, of which the foundation of the United Nations was a symbol. But soon after the end of the war the brutalization continued. The weapons of destruction became ever more powerful; now both sides are able to destroy at least half of each other's population (including most of their educated populations) in one day. Yet the consideration of the possibility of such mass destruction has become commonplace. Many on both sides are fighting to prevent the final act of madness; groups of men and women who follow the tradition of science, of humanism and of hope.

But millions have succumbed to the process of brutalization, and many more are just apathetic, and escape into the trivialities of the day.

The loss of hope and the increasing brutalization are, unfortunately, not the only evils that have befallen Western civilization since 1914. Another cause for the deterioration of Western civilization is connected precisely with its greatest achievements. The industrial revolution has led to a degree of material production which has given the vast majority of the peoples of the West a standard of living which would have seemed unthinkable to most observers a hundred years ago. However, the satisfaction of real and legitimate needs has changed into the creation and satisfaction of a powerful drive, namely, "commodity hunger." Just as depressed individuals often are seized by a compelling desire to buy things or in other cases to eat, modern man has a greedy hunger for possessing and using new things, a hunger which he rationalizes as an expression of his wish for a better life. He claims that the things he buys, if they are not directly enriching to life, help him to save time. Yet he does not know what to do with the time he saves, and spends one part of his income to kill the time he is so proud of having saved.

We see this phenomenon most clearly in the richest country of the world, in the United States. But it is quite clear that the trend in all other countries is the same. The goal everywhere has become maximal production and maximal consumption. The criterion of progress is seen in the figures for consumption. This holds true for the capitalist countries as well as for the Soviet Union. In fact, the rivalry between the two systems seems to center around the question of which can produce a higher level of consumption, rather than a better life. As a result, man in the industrialized countries transforms himself more and more into a greedy, passive consumer. Things are not provided to serve the perfection of man, but man has become the servant of things, as a producer and as a consumer.

The industrial system has had very unfortunate effects in still another direction. The method of production has changed considerably since the beginning of this century. Production, as well as distribution, is organized in big corporations which employ hundreds of thousands of workers, clerks, engineers, salesmen, etc. They are managed by a hierarchically organized bureaucracy, and each person turns into a small—or large—cog in this machine. He lives under the illusion of being an individual—while he has turned into a thing. As a result, we observe an increasing lack of adventurousness, individualism, willingness to make decisions and take risks. The goal is security, to be part of the big powerful machine, to be protected by it, and to feel strong in the symbiotic connection with it. All studies and observation of the younger generation show the same picture: the trend to look for *safe* jobs, not to be concerned so much with high income but rather with satisfactory retirement provisions; the tendency to marry young and to shift quickly from the haven of the parental family to the haven of matrimony; cliché thinking, conformity and obedience to the anonymous authority of public opinion and of the accepted patterns of feeling.

From the fight against the authority of Church, State, and family which characterize the last centuries, we have come back full circle to a new obedience; but this obedience is not one to autocratic persons, but to the organization. The "organization man" is not aware that he obeys; he believes that he only conforms with what is rational and practical. Indeed, disobedience has become almost extinct in the society of organization men, regardless of their ideology. Yet one must remember that the capacity for disobedience is as great a virtue as the capacity for obedience. One must remember that, according to the Hebrew and Greek myths, human history began with an act of disobedience. Adam and Eve, living in the Garden of Eden were still part of nature, as the fetus is in the womb of the mother. Only when they dared to disobey an order were their eyes opened; they recognized each other as strangers and the world outside as strange and hostile. Their act of disobedience broke the primary bond with nature and made them individuals. Disobedience was the first act of freedom, the beginning of human history. Prometheus, stealing the fire of the gods, is another disobedient dissenter. "I would rather be chained to this rock than be the obedient servant of the gods," he said. His act of stealing the fire is his gift to men, thus laying the very basis for civilization. He, like Adam and Eve, was punished for his disobedience; yet he, like them, has made human evolution possible. Man has continued to evolve by acts of disobedience not just in the sense that his *spiritual* development was possible only because there have been men who dared to say "no" to the powers that be in the name of their conscience or of their faith. His *intellectual* development was also dependent on the capacity for being disobedient, disobedient to the authorities who tried to muzzle new thoughts, and to the authority of long-established opinions which declared change to be nonsense.

If the capacity for disobedience constituted the beginning of human history, obedience might cause the end of human history. I am not speaking symbolically or poetically. There is the possibility that the human race will destroy itself and all life on earth within the next ten to fifteen years. There is no rationality or sense in it. But the fact is that while we are living technically in the atomic age, the majority of men live emotionally still in the stone age, including most of those who are in power. If mankind commits suicide, it will be because people will obey those who command them to push the deadly buttons, because they will obey the archaic passions of fear, hate, and greed; because they will obey obsolete clichés of state sovereignty and national honor. The Soviet leaders talk much about revolution, and we in the "free world" talk much about freedom. Yet they discourage disobedience in the Soviet Union explicitly and by force—and we in the free world implicitly and by the more subtle methods of persuasion. There is a difference, and this difference becomes clear if we consider that this praise of disobedience could hardly be published in the Soviet Union while it can be published in the United States. Yet I believe that we are in great danger of being converted into complete organization men, and that means, eventually, into political totalitarianism, unless we regain the capacity to be disobedient and to learn how to doubt.

There is one other aspect of the present situation which I mentioned briefly in the beginning of this book but with which I must now deal more extensively: the problem of a renaissance of humanistic experience.

Sociologically it is easy to see that the evolution of the human race has led from small units like the clan and the tribe through city-states, national states, to world states and world cultures, like the Hellenistic, Roman, Islamic, and modern Western civilization. Yet the difference, as far as human experience is concerned, is not as fundamental as it may seem. The member of the primitive tribe differentiates sharply between the member of his group and the outsider. There are moral laws governing the members of the group, and without such laws no group could exist. But these laws do not apply to the "stranger." When groups grow in size, more people cease to be "strangers" and become "neighbors." Yet in spite of the quantitative change, qualitatively the distinction between the neighbor and the stranger remains. A stranger is not human, he is a barbarian, he is even not fully understandable.

Long before the human race was on the verge of becoming *One World,* socially and economically, its most advanced thinkers had visualized a new human experience, that of *One Man.* The Buddha thought of man as man, as men having the same structure, the same problems, and the same answers, without regard to culture and race. The Old Testament visualized man as being one, bearing the likeness of the One God; the prophets visualized the day when the nations "shall beat their swords into plowshares, and their spears into pruninghooks"; [when] "nation shall not lift up sword against nation, neither shall they learn war any more" (Isaiah 2). They visualized the day when there will be no more "favorite" nations. "In that day shall there be a highway out of Egypt to Assyria, and the Assyrian shall come into Egypt and the Egyptian into Assyria . . . In that day shall Israel be the third with Egypt and with Assyria, even a blessing in the midst of the land: whom the Lord of hosts shall bless saying, Blessed be Egypt my people, and Assyria the work of my hands, and Israel mine inheritance" (Isaiah 19).

Christianity created the concept that the Son of Man became the Son of God—and God himself. Not this or that man, but Man. The Roman Church was a *Catholic* church precisely because it was a supranational, universal church. Classic Greek and Roman thinking arrived independently from Judaeo-Christian thought at the concept of One Man and of natural law rooted in the rights of man, rather than in the necessities of a nation or a state. Antigone sacrifices her life in defense of universal human (natural) law against state law. Zenon had the vision of a universal commonwealth. The Renaissance and Enlightenment enriched the Greek and Judaeo-Christian traditions and developed them further, in humanistic rather than in theological terms. Kant constructed a moral principle valid for all men and outlined the possibility of eternal peace. Schiller wrote (September 27, 1788): "The state is only a result of human forces, only a work of our thoughts, but man is the force of the source itself and the creator of the thought." In *Don Carlos,* Posa speaks "as the deputy of all humanity whose heart beats /For all mankind; his passion was /The world and future generations."

The most complete and profound expression of this humanism appears in the thought of Goethe. His Iphigenia speaks in the voice of humanity, as the classic Antigone did. When the Barbarian king asks her:

> And dost thou think
> That the uncultured Scythian will attend
> The voice of truth and of humanity
> Which Atreus, the Greek, heard not?

she answers:

> 'Tis heard
> By everyone, born 'neath whatever clime,
> Within whose bosom flows the stream of life
> Pure and unhindered.

Goethe wrote (in 1790): "At a time when everybody is busy erecting new Fatherlands, the Fatherland of the man who thinks without prejudice and can rise above his time is nowhere and everywhere."

But in spite of the ideas which the greatest representatives of Western culture held, history took a different path. Nationalism killed humanism. The nation and its sovereignty became the new idols to which the individual succumbed.

In the meantime, however, the world has changed. The revolution of the colonial peoples, communication by air, the radio, etc., have shrunk the globe to the proportions of one continent or, rather, one state as they existed one hundred years ago. The One World which is in the process of being born is, however, not one world because of the friendly and brotherly relations that exist among its various parts, but rather because of the fact that missiles can carry death and destruction to almost any part of the world in a matter of hours. The one world is *one,* so far, inasmuch as it is one potential battlefield, rather than a new system of world citizenship. We live in one world, yet in his feelings and thoughts contemporary man still lives in the nation state. His loyalties are still primarily to sovereign states and not to the human race. This anachronism can only lead to disaster. It is a situation similar to that of the religious wars before religious tolerance and coexistence became an accepted principle of European life.

If the One World is not to destroy itself, it needs a new kind of man—a man who transcends the narrow limits of his nation and who experiences every human being as a neighbor, rather than as a barbarian; a man who feels at home in the world.

Why is this step so difficult? Man's life begins in the womb. Even after birth he is still part of mother, just as primitive man was part of nature. He becomes increasingly aware of himself as separate from others, yet he is deeply drawn to the security and safety of his past. He is afraid of emerging fully as an individual. Mother, the tribe, the family—they all are "familiar." The stranger, the one who is not familiar through the bonds of blood, customs, food, language, is suspected of being dangerous.

This attitude toward the "stranger" is inseparable from the attitude toward oneself. As long as any fellow being is experienced as fundamentally different from myself, as long as he remains a stranger, I remain a stranger to myself too. When I experience myself fully, then I recognize that I am the same as any other human being, that I am the child, the sinner, the saint, the one who hopes and the one who despairs, the one who can feel joy and the one who can feel sadness. I discover that only the thought concepts, the customs, the surface are different, and that the human substance is the same. I discover that I am everybody, and that I discover myself in discovering my fellow man, and vice versa. In this experience I discover what humanity is, I discover the One Man.

Until now the One Man may have been a luxury, since the One World had not yet emerged. Now the One Man must emerge if the One World is to live. Historically speaking, this may be a step comparable with the great revolution which was constituted by the step from the worship of many gods to the One God—or the One No-God. This step was characterized by the idea that man must cease to serve idols, be they nature or the work of his own hands. Man has never yet achieved this aim. He changed the name of his idols and continued serving them. Yet he changed. He made some progress in understanding himself, and tremendous progress in understanding nature. He developed his reason and approached the frontiers of becoming fully human. Yet in this process he developed such destructive powers, that he may destroy civilization before the last step is taken toward constructing a new humanity.

Indeed, we have a rich heritage which waits for its realization. But in contrast to the men of the eighteenth and nineteenth centuries who had an unfailing belief in the continuity of progress, we visualize the possibility that, instead of progress, we may create barbarism or our total destruction. The alternative of socialism or barbarism has become frighteningly real today, when the forces working toward barbarism seem to be stronger than those working against it. But it is not the "socialism" of managerial totalitarianism which will save the world from barbarism. It is the renaissance of humanism, the emergence of a new West which employs its new technical powers for the sake of man, rather than using man for the sake of things; it is a new society in which the norms for man's unfolding govern the economy, rather than the social and political process being governed by blind and anarchic economic interests.

In this struggle for a humanist renaissance Marx's and Freud's ideas are important guideposts. Marx had a much deeper insight into the nature of the social process, and he was much more independent than Freud of the social and political ideologies of his time. Freud had a deeper insight into the nature of the process of human thought, affects, and passions, even though he did not transcend the principles of bourgeois society. They both have given us the intellectual tools to break through the sham of rationalization and ideologies, and to penetrate to the core of individual and social reality.

Regardless of the shortcomings of their respective theories, they have removed mystifying veils which covered over human reality; they have laid the foundations for a new Science of Man; and this new science is badly needed if the Age of Man is to be ushered in—if, to speak with Emerson, things are to cease riding mankind, and if man is to be put into the saddle.

XII

CREDO

I BELIEVE that man is the product of natural evolution; that he is part of nature and yet transcends it, being endowed with reason and self-awareness.

I believe that man's essence is ascertainable. However, this essence is not a substance which characterizes man at all times through history. The essence of man consists in the above-mentioned contradiction inherent in his existence, and this contradiction forces him to react in order to find a solution. Man cannot remain neutral and passive toward this existential dichotomy. By the very fact of his being human, he is asked a question by life: how to overcome the split between himself and the world outside of him in order to arrive at the experience of unity and oneness with his fellow man and with nature. Man has to answer this question every moment of his life. Not only—or even primarily—with thoughts and words, but by his mode of being and acting.

I believe that there are a number of limited and ascertainable answers to this question of existence (the history of religion and philosophy is a catalogue of these answers); yet there are basically only two categories of answers. In one, man attempts to find again harmony with nature by regression to a prehuman form of existence, eliminat-

174

ing his specifically human qualities of reason and love. In the other, his goal is the full development of his human powers until he reaches a new harmony with his fellow man and with nature.

I believe that the first answer is bound to failure. It leads to death, destruction, suffering, and never to the full growth of man, never to harmony and strength. The second answer requires the elimination of greed and ego-centricity, it demands discipline, will, and respect for those who can show the way. Yet, although this answer is the more difficult one, it is the only answer which is not doomed to failure. In fact, even before the final goal is reached, the activity and effort expended in approaching it has a unifying and integrating effect which intensifies man's vital energies.

I believe that man's basic alternative is the choice between life and death. Every act implies this choice. Man is free to make it, but this freedom is a limited one. There are many favorable and unfavorable conditions which incline him—his psychological constitution, the condition of the specific society into which he was born, his family, teachers, and the friends he meets and chooses. It is man's task to enlarge the margin of freedom, to strengthen the conditions which are conducive to life as against those which are conducive to death. Life and death, as spoken of here, are not the biological states, but states of being, of relating to the world. Life means constant change, constant birth. Death means cessation of growth, ossification, repetition. The unhappy fate of many is that they do not make the choice. They are neither alive nor dead. Life becomes a burden, an aimless enterprise, and busyness is the means to protect one from the torture of being in the land of shadows.

I believe that neither life nor history has an ultimate meaning which in turn imparts meaning to the life of the individual or justifies his suffering. Considering the contradictions and weaknesses which beset man's existence it is only too natural that he seeks for an "absolute" which gives him the illusion of certainty and relieves him from conflict, doubt and responsibility. Yet, no god, neither in theological, philosophical or historical garments saves, or condemns man. Only man can find a goal for life and the means for the realization of this goal. He cannot find a saving ultimate or absolute answer but he can strive for a degree of intensity, depth and clarity of experience which gives him the strength to live without illusions, and to be free.

I believe that no one can "save" his fellow man by making the choice for him. All that one man can do for another is to show him the alternatives truthfully and lovingly, yet without sentimentality or illusion. Confrontation with the true alternatives may awaken all the hidden energies in a person, and enable him to choose life as against death. If he cannot choose life, no one else can breathe life into him.

I believe that there are two ways of arriving at the choice of the good. The first is that of duty and obedience to moral commands. This way can be effective, yet one must consider that in thousands of years only a minority have fulfilled even the requirements of the Ten Commandments. Many more have committed crimes when they were presented to them as commands by those in authority. The other way is to develop a taste for and a sense of well-being in doing what is good or right. By taste for well-being, I do not mean pleasure in the Benthamian or Freudian sense. I refer to the sense of heightened aliveness in which I confirm my powers and my identity.

I believe that education means to acquaint the young with the best heritage of the human race. But while much of this heritage is expressed in words, it is effective only if these words become reality in the person of the teacher and in the practice and structure of society. Only the idea which has materialized in the flesh can influence man; the idea which remains a word only changes words.

I believe in the perfectibility of man. This perfectibility means that man *can* reach his goal, but it does not mean that he *must* reach it. If the individual will not choose life and does not grow, he will by necessity become destructive, a living corpse. Evilness and self-loss are as real as are goodness and aliveness. They are the secondary potentialities of man if he chooses not to realize his primary potentialities.

I believe that only exceptionally is a man born as a saint or as a criminal. Most of us have dispositions for good and for evil, although the respective weight of these dispositions varies with individuals. Hence, our fate is largely determined by those influences which mold and form the given dispositions. The family is the most important influence. But the family itself is mainly an agent of society, the transmission belt for those values and norms which a society wants to impress on its members. Hence, the most important factor for the development of the individual is the structure and the values of the society into which he has been born.

I believe that society has both a furthering and an inhibiting function. Only in cooperation with others, and in the process of work, does man develop his powers, only in the historical process does he create himself. But at the same time, most societies until now have served the aims of the few who wanted to use the many. Hence they had to use their power to stultify and intimidate the many (and thus, indirectly, themselves), to prevent them from developing all their powers; for this reason society has always conflicted with humanity, with the universal norms valid for every man. Only when society's aim will have become identical with the aims of humanity, will society cease to cripple man and to further evil.

I believe that every man represents humanity. We are different as to intelligence, health, talents. Yet we are all one. We are all saints and sinners, adults and children, and no one is anybody's superior or judge. We have all been awakened with the Buddha, we have all been crucified with Christ, and we have all killed and robbed with Genghis Khan, Stalin, and Hitler.

I believe that man can visualize the experience of the whole universal man only by realizing his individuality and never by trying to reduce himself to an abstract, common denominator. Man's task in life is precisely the paradoxical one of realizing his individuality and at the same time transcending it and arriving at the experience of universality. Only the fully developed individual self can drop the ego.

I believe that the One World which is emerging can come into existence only if a New Man comes into being —a man who has emerged from the archaic ties of blood and soil, and who feels himself to be the son of man, a citizen of the world whose loyalty is to the human race and to life, rather than to any exclusive part of it; a man who loves his country because he loves mankind, and whose judgment is not warped by tribal loyalties.

I believe that man's growth is a process of continuous birth, of continuous awakening. We are usually half-asleep and only sufficiently awake to go about our business; but we are not awake enough to go about living, which is the only task that matters for a living being. The great leaders of the human race are those who have awakened man from his half-slumber. The great enemies of humanity are those who put it to sleep, and it does not matter whether their sleeping potion is the worship of God or that of the Golden Calf.

I believe that the development of man in the last four thousand years of history is truly awe-inspiring. He has developed his reason to a point where he is solving the riddles of nature, and has emancipated himself from the blind power of the natural forces. But at the very moment of his greatest triumph, when he is at the threshold of a new world, he has succumbed to the power of the very things and organizations he has created. He has invented a new method of producing, and has made production and distribution his new idol. He worships the work of his hands and has reduced himself to being the servant of things. He uses the name of God, of freedom, of humanity, of socialism, in vain; he prides himself on his powers—the bombs and the machines—to cover up his human bankruptcy; he boasts of his power to destroy in order to hide his human impotence.

I believe that the only force that can save us from self-destruction is reason; the capacity to recognize the unreality of most of the ideas that man holds, and to penetrate to the reality veiled by the layers and layers of deception and ideologies; reason, not as a body of knowledge, but as a "kind of energy, a force which is fully comprehensible only in its agency and effects . . ." a force whose "most important function consists in its power to bind and to dissolve." [1] Violence and arms will not save us; sanity and reason may.

I believe that reason cannot be effective unless man has hope and belief. Goethe was right when he said that the deepest distinction between various historical periods is that between belief and disbelief, and when he added that all epochs in which belief dominates are brilliant, uplifting, and fruitful, while those in which disbelief dominates vanish because nobody cares to devote himself to the

---

[1] Ernst Cassirer, *The Philosophy of the Enlightenment* (Boston: Beacon Press, 1955), p. 13.

unfruitful. No doubt the thirteenth century, the Renaissance, the Enlightenment, were ages of belief and hope. I am afraid that the Western World in the twentieth century deceives itself about the fact that it has lost hope and belief. Truly, where there is no belief in man, the belief in machines will not save us from vanishing; on the contrary, this "belief" will only accelerate the end. Either the Western World will be capable of creating a renaissance of humanism in which the fullest developments of man's humanity, and not production and work, are the central issues—or the West will perish as many other great civilizations have.

I believe that to recognize the truth is not primarily a matter of intelligence, but a matter of character. The most important element is the courage to say *no,* to disobey the commands of power and of public opinion; to cease being asleep and to become human; to wake up and lose the sense of helplessness and futility. Eve and Prometheus are the two great rebels whose very "crimes" liberated mankind. But the capacity to say "no" meaningfully, implies the capacity to say "yes" meaningfully. The "yes" to God is the "no" to Caesar; the "yes" to man is the "no" to all those who want to enslave, exploit, and stultify him.

I believe in freedom, in man's right to be himself, to assert himself and to fight all those who try to prevent him from being himself. But freedom is more than the absence of violent oppression. It is more than "freedom from." It is "freedom to"—the freedom to become independent; the freedom to *be* much, rather than to *have* much, or to *use* things and people.

I believe that neither Western capitalism nor Soviet or Chinese communism can solve the problem of the future. They both create bureaucracies which transform man into a thing. Man must bring the forces of nature and of society under his conscious and rational control; but not under the control of a bureaucracy which administers things *and* man, but under the control of the free and associated producers who administer things and subordinate them to man, who is the measure of all things. The alternative is not between "capitalism" and "communism" but between bureaucratism and humanism. Democratic, decentralizing socialism is the realization of those conditions which are necessary to make the unfolding of all man's powers the ultimate purpose.

I believe that one of the most disastrous mistakes in individual and social life consists in being caught in stereotyped alternatives of thinking. "Better dead than red," "an alienated industrial civilization or individualistic preindustrial society," "to rearm or to be helpless," are examples of such alternatives. There are always other and new possibilities which become apparent only when one has liberated oneself from the deathly grip of clichés, and when one permits the voice of humanity, and reason, to be heard. The principle of "the lesser evil" is the principle of despair. Most of the time it only lengthens the period until the greater evil wins out. To risk doing what is right and human, and have faith in the power of the voice of humanity and truth, is more realistic than the so-called realism of opportunism.

I believe that man must get rid of illusions that enslave and paralyze him; that he must become aware of the reality inside and outside of him in order to create a world which needs no illusions. Freedom and independence can be achieved only when the chains of illusion are broken.

I believe that today there is only one main concern: the question of war and peace. Man is likely to destroy all life on earth, or to destroy all civilized life and the values among those that remain, and to build a barbaric, totalitarian organization which will rule what is left of mankind. To wake up to this danger, to look through the double talk on all sides which is used to prevent men from seeing the abyss toward which they are moving is the one obligation, the one moral and intellectual command which man must respect today. If he does not, we all will be doomed.

If we should all perish in the nuclear holocaust, it will not be because man was not capable of becoming human, or that he was inherently evil; it would be because the consensus of stupidity has prevented him from seeing reality and acting upon the truth.

I believe in the perfectability of man, but I doubt whether he will achieve this goal, unless he awakens soon.

> Watchman, what of the night?
> The watchman says:
> Morning comes and also the night
> If you will inquire, inquire:
> Return, come back again.
>
> (Isaiah 21)

ABOUT THE AUTHOR

Erich Fromm was born in Frankfurt, Germany, in 1900. He studied at the Universities of Heidelberg and Munich and at the Psychoanalytic Institute in Berlin. Dr. Fromm taught in Germany, in Mexico where he was Professor of Psychoanalysis at the National University, and in many schools in the United States, including Columbia, Yale, Michigan State and New York Universities, Bennington College, and the William Alanson White Institute of Psychiatry. In his later years he made his residence in Locarno, Switzerland, where he died in 1980. Dr. Fromm is widely known for his work in psychoanalysis, philosophy, political science, and religion. Of his many books, among the most influential are *The Art of Loving, Escape from Freedom, Beyond the Chains of Illusion,* and *The Heart of Man.*

ABOUT THE FOUNDER OF THIS SERIES

Ruth Nanda Anshen, Ph.D., Fellow of the Royal Society of Arts of London, founded, plans, and edits several distinguished book series, including World Perspectives, Religious Perspectives, Credo Perspectives, Perspectives in Humanism, the Science of Culture series, the Tree of Life series, and Convergence. Dr. Anshen is the author of *The Reality of the Devil: Evil in Man,* a study in the phenomenology of evil which examines the interrelationship between good and evil. She has also written and lectured widely on the unity of mind and matter, and on the nature of man and his understanding of his place in the universe. Dr. Anshen is a member of the American Philosophical Association, the History of Science Society, the International Philosophical Society and the Metaphysical Society of America.